A CASE FOR FAITH

A CASE FOR FAITH

Clark H. Pinnock

BETHANY HOUSE PUBLISHERS
MINNEAPOLIS, MINNESOTA 55438
A Division of Bethany Fellowship, Inc.

Previously published as *Reason Enough* by InterVarsity Press.

Published by Bethany House Publishers
A Division of Bethany Fellowship, Inc.
6820 Auto Club Road, Minneapolis, Minnesota 55438

Printed in the United States of America

Library of Congress Cataloging-in-Publication Data

Pinnock, Clark H., 1937-
   A case for faith.

   Previously published: Reason enough Downers Grove, Ill. : InterVarsity Press, c1980.
   1. Apologetics—20th century. I. Title
BT1102.P53   1987   239   86-31676
ISBN 0-87123-953-1

For Dorothy and Sarah
With love and appreciation

Other books by Clark Pinnock

Three Keys to Spiritual Renewal
Set Forth Your Case
A Defense of Biblical Infallibility
Biblical Revelation: The Foundation of Christian Theology
Truth on Fire
Toward a Theology for the Future
Grace Unlimited
The Scripture Principle

Preface   9

Introduction: Is There Reason Enough?   *11*

The Five Circles   *13*
What Is Truth?   *16*
Christian Persuasion   *17*

1 Circle One: The Pragmatic Basis for Faith   *21*

The Humanist Faith   *21*
Our Quest for Meaning   *23*
From Darkness to Light   *25*
The Reasonableness of Belief   *28*
The Ethical Problem   *30*
The Problem of Sin   *32*
Can Life without God Make Sense?   *34*
The End of the Matter   *36*

2 Circle Two: The Experiential Basis for Faith   *39*

A Remarkable Fact   *39*
Unsecular Man   *41*
The Lack of Universality   *43*
The Other Religions   *45*
Religious Experience and the Christian Message   *46*
In Contrast to World-weariness   *49*
What Does It Prove?   *50*
Christian Hedonism?   *54*

3 Circle Three: The Cosmic Basis for Faith   *55*

Natural Theology: The Proclamation of the Skies   *56*
The Marvels of Design   *59*
The Creation of the World   *61*
A Dozen Other Clues   *64*
The Moral Dimension   *66*
The Quest for Intelligibility   *68*
A Steppingstone   *70*

4 Circle Four: The Historical Basis for Faith   *73*

Religion for the Tough-minded   *73*
The Fact of Christ   *75*
Who Then Was Jesus?   *79*
The New Beginning   *84*
The Principle of Analogy   *88*
What Does It Mean?   *89*

5 Circle Five: The Community Basis for Faith   *93*

The Original Revolution   *95*
The Social Impact of the Gospel   *99*
BPGINFWMY   *103*

6 In Case of Doubt   *107*

Pseudoproblems   *109*
Blessings in Disguise: Marx, Freud and Feminism   *111*
Real Difficulties   *114*
Dealing with Doubt   *117*

Conclusion   *119*

Notes   *123*

PREFACE

In every age and cultural setting Christians need to explain to outsiders the reasons for their faith in Christ in terms that make sense. My purpose in writing this book is to communicate with people who are interested in investigating the truth claims made on behalf of the Christian message. Is Christianity, in fact, true? I also want to help believers who from time to time find themselves asking the same question.

In contrast to the secular sixties when I wrote another book in this vein called *Set Forth Your Case*, large numbers of people are turning to faith in response to the gnawing emptiness at the heart of secular life and to the enormous problems that face our global existence today. But faith by itself is not enough if it leads people into vain superstitions and cruel illusions which cannot ultimately sustain life and thought. We must exercise critical judgment in the context of our beliefs, so that the faith we hold is reasonable. We should test it in the light of the knowledge and experience we have at our disposal.

I take the question of truth very seriously. I do not believe we need to commit ourselves without reasonable grounds. I am also convinced that the essential reasons for the Christian faith can be explained in understandable language and in a way that does not require special study. I hope, therefore, to present a fairly comprehensive evidential picture so that all of us will be able to discern the boundaries surrounding this subject area and many of the leading issues on and below its surface.

I recognize, of course, that there are many ways to argue on behalf of the Christian faith. No two people will go about it exactly the same way. I sincerely hope, however, that my efforts will help those who are probing the question of commitment to Christ and move them closer to taking that step.[1]

I am writing, then, for those who do not believe and for those who experience difficulties in their believing. "Wisdom is calling out. Reason is making herself heard" (Proverbs 8:1). As one who struggles with faith in the setting of the secular university, I think I am sensitive to the pervasive influence of secularity in the modern world. I know what it is like to feel that we live in a relative and contingent universe and can do without God and salvation. I do not have to imagine the doubts and uncertainties people feel when the demands of the gospel confront them. But I am also convinced that the Christian world view is adequate intellectually, factually and morally. And I delight in this opportunity to share with others the evidences I have discovered.

The issues at stake are important not only for life in this world but also, I believe, for life beyond death. They are momentous enough to demand and deserve careful thought and consideration by all of us. So let us *think about believing* together, and let me share why I think there is reason enough to put our trust in Christ.[2]

Introduction

Is There Reason Enough?

Some people become Christians without ever thinking about it. They accept Christ as their Lord and Savior because of an emotional appeal that seems to meet their needs, but they never really ask whether what they are doing is reasonable. The thought never occurs to them. Because of this many thinking people wonder whether Christianity isn't all faith, that is, totally devoid of rational justification.

I sympathize with this. If one looked only on the surface of much of today's Christianity, I think the feeling would be justified. But there is, after all, a depth to the faith of many Christians which is not to be separated from reason and long, hard thought. In fact, when we examine the history of Christianity, we discover that Jesus himself had a respect for human intelligence.

Once John the Baptist was in prison and doubted his own faith in Jesus as the Messiah that God had promised to send.

So John sent his disciples to Jesus asking for a word of confirmation. But Jesus did not just answer yes and leave John to believe it or not. Rather he told them to return to their master and tell him what they saw—the blind were now seeing, the lame were walking, the sick were healed, the poor were hearing the good news (Matthew 11:2-6). And Jesus charged them to yield to the weight of the evidence.

When others questioned him about his claim to be the Son of God and equal with God, Jesus appealed to various witnesses, including the earlier word of John the Baptist, the evidence of the miracles, and the testimony of the Old Testament Scriptures (John 5:17-18, 31-40). This attitude to the value of evidence and reason permeates the New Testament. Each of the Gospels was written to provide evidence on behalf of the Christian proclamation or to answer questions which had arisen in people's minds about it.

Matthew, for example, wants to prove that Jesus is the promised Messiah, and so he summons up the rich prophetic witness of the ancient Scriptures. Luke tells us at the very outset of his work that he purposes to convince Theophilus of the truth and certainty of the message (Luke 1:1-4). The practice of the apostle Paul in his efforts to spread the faith was to engage people in reasoned argument concerning the Word of God (Acts 17:2-4; 19:8-10). Almost all of the New Testament books were written to exhibit the credibility of the Christian message and to answer questions that had arisen in the minds of critics and sympathizers alike.[1]

I recognize that there are those who think that religion cannot and should not be supported by any rational means. Some of them hold this opinion because they have not yet been convinced that reasons for faith exist, and others because of the influence of existential styles of thinking. Faith, they hold, is void of all security, whether intuitive or intellectual, and any attempt to bolster it with reasoned argument is self-contradictory.

But I don't think that faith can bypass the truth question so easily. Rather I am committed to appealing to reason to try to persuade those yet unconvinced to make a decision for Jesus Christ. Faith according to the Bible does not involve a rash decision made without reflection or a blind submission in the face of an authoritarian claim. It is the act of wholehearted trust in the goodness and promises of the God who confronts us with his reality and gives us ample reason to believe that he is there.

It is perfectly in order before making such a commitment to scrutinize the alternatives and weigh all the issues. I see reasons for faith serving as a road map helping us determine where we wish to go and showing us how to get there. One of the things that makes the Christian message an option for us today is its ability to show us reason enough to be committed to Christ.

The Five Circles

I have organized the argument of this book into what I call five circles of credibility, that is, five subject areas or categories of evidence which support in a complementary way the Christian understanding of reality and Christ's claim on our lives. All of them are referred to in the Bible, and all of them have been used with regularity in the literature of Christian persuasion for the past two thousand years. A brief summary of these five arguments and evidences will give an overview of the chapters that follow.

Circle one points to the practical value of the Christian faith and hence is called the *pragmatic* basis for faith. All of us need to believe that our lives have dignity and worth, and the gospel gives us the necessary basis for believing that they do. It satisfies a basic human need. The hunger after meaning is a deep existential drive within the human heart, and the gospel can satisfy that hunger by supplying the solid basis for confidence in the worthwhileness of life. Circle one is a basic argument for faith which does not presuppose a religious interest but addresses the question which ordinary life always raises.

Circle two looks at the *experiential* dimension of religious and Christian faith. Although often downplayed as "subjective," the evidence of religious experience is universal and impressive, and cannot be left out of the evidential picture. There is a host of high quality reports and reporters, not the least of whom is Jesus himself, and the relevance of their testimonies to the fundamental desire of the human heart to be in touch with the creative ground of reality makes this circle crucial. Religious experience is a fact about our world which cannot just be swept aside and ignored. The offer of a vibrant relationship with a loving Father is central to the gospel and is an exciting possibility that deserves to be considered.

Circle three focuses on the *cosmic* (or metaphysical) basis for faith. Here we broaden the horizon of our investigation to consider the mystery of the universe itself over and above its strictly human dimension. Mankind has always been engaged in a quest after the intelligibility not only of his own existence but of the world, a world which is full of marvelous wonders that cry out to be accounted for. Circle three shows us that belief in God makes rational sense of the world and fulfills the deep human desire to explain and understand it. In my view science has not made belief any harder or unbelief any easier but has if anything provided us with fresh evidences of the existence of God. As the psalmist says, "How clearly the sky reveals God's glory! How plainly it shows what he has done!" (Psalm 19:1).

Circle four which deals with the *historical* basis for faith is particularly important to our presentation for two reasons. First, the gospel is centrally concerned with God's intervention in the history of the world in the life of ancient Israel and especially in the career of Jesus of Nazareth. Second, circle four focuses precisely on the object of Christian faith, the person of Christ himself. The first three circles prepare us to take seriously what the gospel says. But they do not by themselves identify the gospel as the unique message of salvation that is historically mediated to us.

In an attempt to convince King Agrippa about the gospel of Christ, the apostle Paul reminded him that the facts underlying the message were not "hidden away in a corner" (Acts 26:26). They were capable of being investigated because they occurred on the stage of verifiable history. To the Athenians he even said, in discussing the coming judgment the whole world would one day face, that God "has given proof of this to everyone by raising that man [Jesus] from death" (Acts 17:31). In the last analysis the decision to be a Christian will be a decision about the person and history of Jesus the Christ.

Circle five has to do with the way Jesus' followers have lived. A new human reality was created by the resurrection of Jesus and the outpouring of the Spirit. There is, therefore, a *community* basis for faith that calls attention to Jesus' promise of personal and social healing. Although the record of Christians is not flawless, there is good evidence that the gospel can create new community. The promise and the reality are there. Those who long to belong to the family of God should be drawn by this evidence.

A glance at the five circles will show that I believe the gospel is "true" in various ways. It is the true end to our quest for meaning and our quest for the intelligibility of the world, true to the religious longings of our heart, true to the biblical record, and true to the moral intuition that we need a new kind of human community on this groaning planet. The five circles together provide a comprehensive structure of evidence that goes a long way toward justifying Christianity's claim to truth. Since the Christian faith addresses so many aspects of human life, it only is natural that evidence for its truth will be found in a variety of settings and that these various circles will interact with each other in a complementary way creating a cumulative effect on the mind. One circle appeals more to practical relevance and another more to intellectual comprehension, but both contribute to an adequate case for the gospel.

The image of the circle is not the only one possible. Circles designate broad areas which contain evidences of a specific kind. We could, however, speak of them as lines of argument directing our understanding to the true object of faith, or as points in a lawyer's presentation which are adduced to convince a judge and jury.

Whatever image is used, the main point is that a rich selection of Christian evidences exists and that these various indicators of truth work together to lead us to a reasonable conclusion.

What Is Truth?

This book will not be burdened with a lengthy discussion of epistemology, the question of how we know what we know. But I do want to outline the model of rationality I am assuming. The fact is that I hold to the way of knowing which everyone of us accepts in his speech and actions.

First, we gain our knowledge of reality through our interaction with the external world. Of course, I am fully aware of certain assumptions that are made in this belief: for example, that an external world actually exists and that the impressions formed in our minds by it correspond to the nature of the reality outside. These common-sense beliefs are hard to prove or disprove. But they underlie all our being and knowing in such a fundamental way that they may be said to be inescapable if not self-evident.

Skepticism in knowledge may be a nice game to play, but there is no way one can live on the basis of it. Of course, our perceptual knowledge is not flawless or complete. Nevertheless, there is no other comparable avenue for obtaining information about the external world, and it is one I certainly propose to travel along with you as a reader. In fact, the glory of the Christian message is that it fits with the relevant facts of our experience and can be verified in an empirical way.

Second, I assume that the only way we can draw reliable conclusions from what we perceive is by thinking consistently and coherently about the data we encounter. Logical thinking is the practice and art of seeing correctly the relationships which exist between the items of observation and the truth we already possess. To take an illustration, it would be logical to conclude that, if a pencil lies to the right of a pen on a table, and a ruler lies to the right of the pencil on the same table, the pencil must lie between the pen and the ruler. It could not be otherwise. The truth concluded is implied by the information at our disposal already and only needed to be drawn out.

We could not make any progress in knowing if we refused to accept the significance of the data at hand. We would find it impossible to make any sense when we talked and communication would break down because it rests on a foundation of logical reasoning. We shall certainly try to observe the requirements of logic in this book, and not draw any inferences illogically from the facts we have.

What it comes down to is this. I do not want to make any special demands in the area of knowledge. I have no hidden assumptions, no special philosophy. My contention is that the truth claim of the Christian gospel can be checked out in the ordinary ways we verify the things we know. In fact, the issues can be tested by ordinary intellects not blessed with brilliance or advanced study. Although the arguments I will touch on can be discussed in the rarified atmosphere of philosophic abstraction, and need to be discussed there, they can also be unfolded in untechnical language for ordinary people.

Christian Persuasion
I see my task as that of Christian persuasion. I am in the role of a fair-minded lawyer seeking to convince you the jury of the truth of the Christian message through the presentation of

the evidences at my disposal. I do not expect to convince you
of it through the overwhelming impact of one line of argument or piece of evidence. Rather I will be inviting you to let
the pieces fit together in your mind. I am asking you to follow
me as I attempt to guide you to the truth. Along the way I
will be pointing out the clues I think you ought to be noticing.
I hope it will result in your coming to the place where you
acknowledge, as I do, that Jesus Christ is Lord.

I am not aiming at rational proof, but rather at a testing of
faith in the light of knowledge which will enable you to take
that step of commitment without sacrificing your intellect. We
will be dealing here with reasonable probabilities. No world
view offers more than that, and Christianity offers nothing
less. There will come a day I believe when God will reveal his
glory in an unmistakable way and there will no longer be any
room for doubt and hesitation. But that day is not yet, and in
the meantime we work with reasonable probabilities which,
while they do not create or compel belief, do establish the
credible atmosphere in which faith can be born and can grow.

I personally see it as one way in which the Lord protects
our cognitive and personal freedom. If it is love that he desires
to give and to receive, it makes sense to me that he would offer
it in such a way that we would remain free to accept or reject
the offer. Such would hardly be the case if God thundered at
us from heaven. Therefore, he approaches us gently with
clues and reminders of who he is as if to woo and win us.

There is, however, a complicating factor. When we face a factual question in ordinary life, we can come to a verdict without
being personally involved. But the more the question touches
the deep issues of life, and the more you are personally involved in the outcome, the stickier the mental operation becomes. It is harder to decide an issue of life and death in a state
of disinterested detachment. Furthermore, the kind of evidence that counts toward a moral and spiritual decision, while
still factual, involves much more evaluation and reflection.

Since we cannot avoid this problem, we might as well face up to it from the start. The stakes involved in the gospel could not be higher, and the decision that is called for involves the whole person. Therefore, thinking about it cannot be quite the same as thinking about the menu for tonight's supper. Nevertheless, the issues we are considering are basic to human existence and have to be faced, however delicate they may be. We will, then, try to confront them as far as possible in the context of critical thought and personal openness.

Chapter 1

Circle One: The Pragmatic Basis for Faith

All of us need to believe that our lives have dignity and worth. So the first circle of credibility shows how the Christian faith supplies the basis for believing this.

The Humanist Faith

For many people in touch with the cultural directions of our time humanism is the framework which appears to sustain and promote the dignity and worth of human life. Originally the term *humanism* was used to refer to a liberalizing movement in fourteenth-century Italy which stood for the values of classical learning including tolerance and the freedom of ideas. It was not opposed to the Christian faith, but to authoritarianism in religion which suppressed personal liberty. The term today, however, stands for something narrower: humanism as a secular world view in opposition to traditional beliefs.

Modern humanism takes a number of forms—Marxist humanism, existential humanism, optimistic humanism—and it represents an important alternative to the position I am advancing. Two "Humanist Manifestos" (1933 and 1973) have been issued in the Anglo-American context, and it will serve our purpose well if I indicate something of their thrust.[1]

First, they are an effort to supply human life with meaning, purpose and direction without having to resort to any religious ideas or authorities. Since there is no god to save us, it is up to man to save himself. Although for most people in the past and even today life is given deep meaning through religious symbols, humanism in this sense proposes to replace religion with its own substitute "theology."

Second, this humanism, while recognizing that the Christian faith appeals to some basic human needs, contends that it is not a rational belief but an illusion produced by wishful thinking. As such we ought not to give in to it. (The reader will already be aware that I agree that our beliefs need to be rationally based and only disagree that the Christian faith is not rational.)

Third, humanism holds that man (male and female) is not a created being but part of an evolving nature, completely on its own and having to work out its own salvation as best it may. Humanist Manifesto I is more optimistic about this happening than is Manifesto II, but there is no lapse in the belief that the values and resources for the task have to arise from within the human race.

All in all, humanism is very much at home in the twentieth century and is well represented in the universities, in the wider culture and often in churches as well. It is a worthy challenge to the Christian who is advocating the truth of the gospel. Both the humanist and the believer stand on some common ground in that both wish to preserve the dignity of the *human person* in the face of serious threats to it. The issue that divides them has to do with the *basis* of this common commitment. Can this concern for human life be best sustained on the basis of secular humanism or in the framework of Christian belief?

Both parties recognize, I think, the importance of this by no means academic question. If there was a time when belief in the worthwhileness of life could be taken for granted, that time has passed. It is being subjected to a series of savage attacks that require us to provide more than a casual intuitive rationale for it. Before the work of Galileo, Darwin, Freud and Skinner, it was easier to think of ourselves as special, important, free and purposeful. But now we are realizing afresh just how insignificant we are in an expanding universe. We hear on every hand that we are the product of a freak accident and the struggle for survival, that we are more like puppets at the mercy of impersonal forces we do not control than the personal agents we thought we were. With such a barrage our easygoing assumptions about the dignity and worth of life have been shattered and many of us feel the wrenching loss of deep meaningfulness. No longer can we cling to the naive hope for meaning; we are driven to explore the foundations.

Our Quest for Meaning

Animals, it seems, come into the world equipped with an impressive set of instincts to guide their behavior and do not seem troubled by the problem of meaning. We as human beings on the other hand reveal a tremendous need to interpret and understand the world and our place in it. We long for a basic meaning system which can interpret the world for us and place the experiences of our life in meaningful perspective. Religion historically has provided the rationale and has made sense of our existence. It has focused attention upon the most fundamental dimensions in the meaning system because it attempts to deal with the most basic and puzzling questions that arise. That is why religion has been central to human life from the beginning of recorded history and why it is likely to continue to exist long after the current phase of secularity has passed.

Religion is the audacious effort to conceive of the entire world as humanly significant; it is rooted in a fundamental human drive toward meaning.[2] When it happens that the interpretability of the universe collapses for people, when they can no longer find coherence and meaning for their lives and do not know who they are or why they are alive, they begin to be immersed in darkness and chaos and desperately need to find something they can believe in and norms which they can follow.

We are experiencing just such a loss of meaning in our time as a result of the demise of Christian faith on the one hand and the failure of the alternatives on the other. According to humanism, for example, a man or a woman comes into the world devoid of any inherent worth, meaning or direction, entirely on their own. There is no larger purposive order in which their lives participate. There is no significance or value for them which they do not create for themselves. They are driven logically to sympathize with Macbeth: "Life is a tale, told by an idiot, full of sound and fury, signifying nothing." At the heart of reality, where the believer finds the Lord, there is darkness and a vacuum. Small wonder we are seeing a crisis of human values, a great deal of aimlessness, inner emptiness and boredom.

I have always appreciated the frank honesty of H. J. Blackham, formerly director of the British Humanist Association, who posed the great problem to his own position as "the pointlessness of it all." How can one escape from the "unyielding despair" of Bertrand Russell, the nihilism of Friedrich Nietzsche and the absurdity of Jean Paul Sartre if at the foundations of our existence there is nothing but blind chance?[3] There is indeed a certain bleakness to humanism, for God has been removed and nothing comparable has yet been found to take his place.

It is easy for believers to forget this, sustained as they are by such powerful symbols of hope: the love of the Father, the plan of salvation, the coming of the kingdom and everlasting life. But they must not allow themselves to forget it for the sake of those who lack these supports and are searching for these foundations. Christians who have been converted early in their lives and never go through the experience of existential darkness before entering into the light of God's coming kingdom have much to learn about these feelings of despair and doubt.

From Darkness to Light

To illustrate this existential darkness we need only examine a classic of the modern theater, *Waiting for Godot* by Samuel Beckett. The basic yearning for meaning and fulfillment is here symbolized by Godot who it is hoped will come and save the situation. The only meaningful activity to undertake in the meantime is to stand and wait for him. Unless he comes, nothing will have any significance. Of course Godot does not come, and hope is indefinitely postponed and unfulfilled. Life is seen to be tragic and futile, drained of real significance. Beckett understands, I think, the meaning of the "death of God" in our life and culture. The loss of faith is no trivial passing from illusion to rationality. It is in fact a revolutionary shift in consciousness: we move out of an orientation in which the world is held together and makes sense and into an orientation where nothingness and desolation cast their shadow across our path. Unbelieving man awakens to find himself unable to experience meaningfulness in a universe indifferent to his needs and ultimately meaningless.

Omitted from the Ten Commandments of the Old Testament, surprisingly enough, is any explicit condemnation of atheism. Attention is directed towards those who have their loyalty wrongly placed, those who regard one god as good as any other and those who believe in God but do nothing about it. But there is no prohibition of atheism as such. From a historical standpoint we could say it is because the challenge in the second millennium B.C. was polytheism not atheism. But from an existential standpoint we may detect another explanation. Atheism is not a serious threat to faith because if it is taken seriously it will make people sad! As soon as they reflect upon its implications on their lives, lived out as they must then be in the context of a meaningless universe, exposing them to the almost inevitable feeling of futility and emptiness, atheism will lose its attraction.

So long as it is not an intellectual pose but a stance seriously adopted, atheism must open up a person to doubt and despair. It needs little threat of punishment or condemnation when it carries on its own shoulders such bitter implications. It practically bars a person from ever hoping to get satisfactory answers to the great questions life raises: Who am I? Where did I come from? What can I know? What shall I do? What may I hope?

The loss of faith in the West has left in disarray some essential perceptions about the meaning of life, and, almost predictably, into the vacuum have sprung all manner of substitute beliefs, not only in the form of strange new cults and superstitions the newspapers love to report, but also in the form of intellectually powerful systems of thought which are bidding for the place which Christian theology once occupied.

Marx and Freud, for example, can be seen in these terms. Each of them has devoted considerable talent and effort to construct a life and world view to fill up the vacuum left by the "death of God." They offer us surrogate theologies, suited to secular thinking and intended to capture the allegiance of post-Christian men and women. That they are antireligious should not blind us to the fact that they offer new mythologies, profoundly religious in nature and scope and aimed at replacing traditional religion in modern culture.

Marxism, for example, is a highly visionary messianic and utopian antitheology, promising salvation to the whole world. It presents a breathtaking historical saga stretching from creation to consummation, from man's fall into class conflict through his progressive emancipation on to the millennium of perfect justice. Marx saw himself as a new Moses, or rather Prometheus, leading an enslaved humanity into the new Canaan. He is breathless with the desire to tell us of the inevitable withering away of the state and the coming of a peaceful world without strife or class conflict.

Marx has taken the biblical symbols and transposed them onto the historical plane, but the system remains profoundly religious, which explains, too, the kind of commitment it can inspire. For my part, I think Marx's prophecy of the new Eden is an illusion. Instead of bringing greater humanization, it has brought systematic terror on a new scale. But if it has failed, it is not the failure only of an economic theory, but of an essentially theological vision, designed to meet the needs we are speaking about.

With Freud, too, we are dealing with a highly mythological and religious surrogate theology. That is especially obvious in the rich use Freud makes of myths in his work. Some of his basic notions did not arise out of controlled experiments but from an imaginative leap of faith. The evidence, if we may call it that, for his highly original view that every tiny male child is eager to kill his father and jump into bed with his mother, is provided by the Greek myth of Oedipus. Time and again instead of citing clinical data for a position, Freud will appeal instead to myth and literature, giving the distinct impression not of scientific theorizing but of religious speculation. Like Marx, Freud saw himself as a new Moses, a destined leader, often betrayed by his closest friends and opposed by the charlatans of prejudice. Though original and fruitful in many ways, Freud's work bears the marks of theology and mythology, and both he and Marx are responding

to the felt need of new foundations to sustain meaningful
life in the absence of God.

The Reasonableness of Belief

The question of God is raised for people today, not so much
in the old form, "Does God exist?" as in a new context, "Does
life have meaning?" Belief in God is related to the basic
human drive toward meaning. God is the rational basis for a
person's hope and confidence in the worthwhileness of his
life.

Peter Berger uses the illustration of a young child waking
up frightened in the night after a bad dream and finding
itself surrounded by darkness. In terror it cries out to its
mother for the comfort and reassurance of her presence,
and she communicates love and security to her child. She
assures it that all is well, there is no need to be afraid, everything is in order and the child drops off to sleep again.

A simple everyday occurrence, but it raises a deeper question too. Are we justified in assuming the stance of trust and
assurance which the mother instinctively adopted? Does
reality deserve our trust? Is the human propensity to suppose
that the world is ordered and even gracious, an assumption
which underlies much of what we do, well founded? As one
who believes in God, I think it is. God himself undergirds the
confidence that reveals itself in dozens of actions in ordinary
life such as in the behavior of that mother. If God did not
exist, there would be no basis for such gestures of hope. But
if he does exist, the situation is transformed.[4]

Alongside this basic confidence in the trustworthiness of
reality can be placed man's propensity to hope. We are all
of us creatures of hope, always taking thought for the limit-
less future which is our goal. Blaise Pascal put it this way:

> We do not rest satisfied with the present. We anticipate the
> future as too slow in coming, as if in order to hasten its
> course; or we recall the past, to stop its too rapid flight.

So imprudent are we that we wander in the times which are not ours, and do not think of the only one which belongs to us. . . . We scarcely ever think of the present; and if we think of it, it is only to take light from it to arrange the future. . . . The past and present are our means; the future alone is our end. So we never live, but we hope to live; and, as we are always preparing to be happy, it is inevitable that we should never be so.[5]

But however dark the prospects seem, we are not dismayed by the future. We continue to hope against hope that our efforts are not doomed to final frustration. We hold on to the significance we believe our lives have. Human life is filled with gestures of hope even in defiance of the direst threats. There even seems to be a death-refusing hope at the center of our humanity.

From a humanist standpoint such hope is an illusion. Death is to be accepted as the natural end of man. We cannot hope beyond death, except in terms of the ongoing historical process on earth. Death must rather be accepted with equanimity as marking the end of one's contribution to the stream of life. There is no future for a person as an individual, and even for the race there is only final destruction in a universe in ruins, as Russell put it. Our own life and the life of the race is bound to become extinct: there is nothing ultimately to hope for or believe in.

But there are a number of objections to this point of view. For one thing it is elitest. It makes a modicum of sense to the few who have succeeded in this life, to the small educated and affluent minority of mankind from which humanists in the West usually draw their numbers. But it is hardly so satisfactory when applied to the majority of the race for whom life in the world as it is at present is neither fulfilling nor joyful, in whose lives the potential for human fulfillment has hardly begun because of the struggle to feed and clothe themselves. In this context the religious hope for life after death

*hmm...
what of
hope now.*

makes a very great deal of sense. The process begun in this
life can continue. If humanism is right in saying that we were
born to achieve happiness, then the fact is that we die too
soon. Our process toward fulfillment is cut off almost as soon
as it starts. It makes more sense to think of life as a stage in a
moral journey which does not end at death.

The Christian message is much more optimistic than humanism. While the latter must view the human destiny as
irredeemably tragic, the gospel asserts that life has meaning
within the divine plan which includes the promise of ultimate
fulfillment and joy. Because of God's love for people, all
shall be well for those that want it so. The hope man feels
within him and which he manifests in a host of ways is indeed
justified. We have a right to say no to death because a God of
hope gives us ground for our trusting.[6] What we need in contemporary culture is a fresh vision and experience of human
life as the gospel understands it, a positive view which sees it
participating in the purposive divine order and sustained by
the love of God.

The Ethical Problem
Living as we do in a world full of suffering and injustice, one
of the common concerns of humanist and Christian alike is
the question of what we are morally expected to do in response to human need. What is it to be moral? And why
should we be moral?

The humanist faces a serious problem here. Since a person's life in this world is his basic tangible value, any action
which threatens or does not advance this possession is irrational. It is hard for me to see why I should ever set any moral
obligation above the ends that serve my own self-interest. How
could a challenge to perform something self-sacrificing ever
have an intelligible claim upon me?

I am not arguing that humanists always act selfishly or
Christians unselfishly, as logic might suggest, but trying to

probe the rational foundations of our ethical response. Ethics arise out of our beliefs concerning what is ultimately real, and it would seem to follow in the case of a humanist that his behavior must be governed by what is to his own advantage in the long run. The morality of self-sacrifice, so much admired by both humanists and Christians, would seem to be irrational on that basis. It is not rationally defensible in terms of humanistic philosophy.

Take the case of the ordinary ant. The ant, it seems, plays a role in the ant colony which is remarkable for its altruism. It gives itself over completely in the service of the ant community. As far as we know, it is disposed to do so by instinct and exercises no personal choice in the matter. Imagine an ant, possessed of the intelligence and freedom enjoyed by a humanist, reflecting upon his life and the demand to sacrifice himself on behalf of the group. Is our enlightened ant likely to embrace voluntarily his own self-destruction? I think not. What reason could he give for doing so? Why opt for the common good when his own brief life is all he has?

We are talking about the rational basis for moral actions, and it is difficult to see how humanism can justify what both humanist and Christian would consider moral action, when that action contravenes personal advantage. Ethics seems to require beliefs not themselves ethical but rather religious in order to function. On the whole I would not criticize the content of humanist ethics so much as their lack of a rational basis.

The philosopher Kant was right long ago to notice that moral activity implies a religious dimension.[7] The atheist Nietzsche also saw the point and argued forcefully that the person who gives up belief in God must be consistent and give up Christian morals as well, because the former is the foundation of the latter. He had nothing but contempt for fellow humanists who refused to see that Christian morality cannot survive the loss of its theological moorings except as habit or lifeless tradition. As Ayn Rand also sees so clearly, love of the neighbor cannot be rationally justified within the framework of secular humanism.[8] Love for one's neighbor is an ethical implication of the Christian position. This suggests to me that the world's deepest problem is not economic or technological, but spiritual and moral. What is missing is the vision of reality that can sustain the neighbor-oriented lifestyle that is so urgently needed in our world today.

Another way to show the religious dimensions of morality is to reflect on the feelings that arise in us when confronted by the horrendous evil depicted in the film and television series of the *Holocaust*. In that event we encounter monstrous atrocities against humanity that violate every human right of man, giving rise to a feeling of outrage, revulsion and disgust. Here were deeds so monstrously evil that they cried out to heaven for a retribution beyond the power of any human court. In that case even people who under normal circumstances might tend to excuse antisocial behavior as the result of social conditioning did not do so but expressed their unconditional condemnation at so absolute an evil.

Although agreeing with such sentiments, I must ask as a Christian why it is we have such feelings. Is there in fact a judgment in the universe that will put right such unrequited evil? Is morality after all something more than social convention and rooted in the nature of things? Here again the deeper dimensions of morality begin to appear.

The Christian faith can make sense out of these moral gestures. It gives us the basis for viewing each other as brothers and sisters. Created in the image of God, all people possess dignity and worth. Humanism can give us no such assurances.

The Problem of Sin
I wish to raise one other issue in connection with moral experience. A persistent tendency in humanism has been to regard man as basically good and to contemplate the future in rosy

terms. As Julian Huxley once said, "What we have faith in is the capabilities and possibilities of man." But, we must ask, how rational is such confidence?

Humanism prides itself on being empirical, but here it ignores the overwhelming evidence that there is something drastically wrong with human behavior. This humanist belief in the inherent goodness of man is surely refuted by any close study of human life. Although we are capable of generous and loving actions, it is also apparent that we all love ourselves more than we should. On every hand we are confronted with the results of morally twisted actions in the form of alienation, violence and pain. The condition of the spirit which psychologists have to deal with most is moral failure and the awareness of guilt. What makes the future so uncertain is not the fear that technology will fail us but that mankind will prove unable to respond to the moral challenges before it.

It may be that the Christian conviction about human sin has been overstated at times, particularly by the Augustinian tradition. Nevertheless, it is an insight which is highly relevant to our understanding of the world.[9] And, more important still, it is accompanied by the promise of redemption which speaks of pardon, reconciliation with God and new life in the Spirit. Faith means deliverance from obsessive self-centeredness and the freedom to love God and other people based on a resource outside of ourselves.

Indeed the Incarnation and the plan of redemption through the cross of Christ deal with our human moral depravity at a profound level. For God places such value upon us, sinful though we undoubtedly are, that he was willing to give his Son up to a cruel death on our behalf. Out of the darkness of our guilt comes a word of grace that despite everything God still loves us. Surely this is a major basis for the dignity and worthwhileness of our human lives.

In short, humanism fails to offer us an adequate substitute for belief and trust in God. However hard we try, we cannot give ourselves the meaning we crave. We cannot resolve the dilemmas arising in the moral sphere. The gospel on the other hand offers a foundation that cannot be shaken and the promise of salvation and hope.

Can Life without God Make Sense?

Does everyone in fact feel this drive toward meaning on which the first circle rests? How is it that there are those who do not seem to ask this question? In reply I would say that people find themselves at different places in relation to it.

Obviously there are many who do face up to the issue and conduct a search for meaning. Writers and artists articulate for the wider public their explorations along this line. But then there are others on whom the question has not yet settled in full force. Many of them have uncomplicated assumptions about meaning and take a great deal for granted. If life has been good to them, they probably have some personal goals—in their job or marriage—which give them enough satisfaction that the question of deeper meaning seems a bit remote. Unfortunately, however, the realities of life have a way of ganging up on a person with shallow assumptions. Something almost always comes along to shatter the dream and raise the issue of meaning for them.

The reason for this is simple: Happiness based on worldly security alone is endlessly vulnerable to the "slings and arrows of outrageous fortune" which may come in the form of illness or inflation or the loss of a loved one. There are all manner of threats to the meaning of our lives both internal and external which can conspire to destroy it if it is inadequately grounded.

What the Christian faith offers us is a structure of deeper meaning based upon the love of the Father which is not vulnerable to destruction. As Paul says, "There is nothing in all creation that will ever be able to separate us from the love of God which is ours through Christ Jesus our Lord" (Romans

8:39). In other words, I am not saying a person should not try to find meaning in the good things of life, but simply that he *cannot* find it at the level required in the realm of material security. The goodness and worthwhileness of life will always be threatened until it is located within the vision of an intelligible and purposive order of significance and meaning that cannot be shaken.

We might say that when the word *God* is used, one thing it has reference to is what Schubert M. Ogden calls "the objective ground in reality itself of our ineradicable confidence in the final worth of our existence."[10] Put in that way we can see that the question is not basically whether or not God exists. Rather, it is the most central question we can ask in our lives, the question that underlies all the others: What gives us the possibility of trusting in the goodness of reality and the goodness of our lives if not belief in the God who created and sustains all things in his plan? In other words, if a good and compassionate God who created and cares for his creation does not exist, can life ultimately have any meaning?

To take it one step further, I would suggest that we reflect on our attitudes and actions. Do they not imply this very confidence, even if we have not actually taken the step of explicit faith in God? There is a sense in which the decision to believe renders explicit the seeds of faith already present, implicit in the confidence humanists and Christians both manifest toward the goodness and worthwhileness of life. By virtue of continuing to live and act, even the atheist shows he must in *some* sense believe in God and cannot in *every* sense deny him.

The apostle Paul quotes a piece of Stoic poetry which says, "In him we live and move and exist" (Acts 17:28). Those who do not believe in God often seem to think that it is fairly easy to stay distant from him, and Christians very often support them in their opinion. But as Paul also said a little earlier, "God is actually not far from any one of us" (17:27). Of course it is easy to deny God verbally. What I am saying is that it is not at all easy to deny him in the living out of life because only the existence of God can adequately support the meaning of life. Confessing the atheist's creed is certainly possible; but living consistently on the basis of it is practically impossible.

What I am asking you as a reader to do, then, is to clear up this inconsistency by the decision to trust in God and to bring about harmony between your explicit beliefs and the underlying confidence in life's meaning that you sense.[11] Should you decide in the other direction, to bring about consistency by working your unbelief in God more deeply into the fabric of your everyday life, I predict great sadness and self-destruction in this life and in the life to come.

The End of the Matter

To put it in a nutshell the Christian message makes it possible for us to have confidence in the dignity and worth of human life. It tells us who we are, created in the image of God and loved with everlasting love. It gives us faith and hope for the living of life. On every hand today people are being reduced to a set of conditioned reflexes and biological responses and treated as though they were punch cards travelling through the entrails of a computer. When human beings are devalued in this way, everything in life and in society begins to go wrong. I feel it is my responsibility as a Christian to speak out against this dehumanization process and explain to any who will listen what reality looks like and what life is like when the God of the gospel is trusted. The first circle of credibility is designed to bring out the deep practical importance of trusting in God.

But would Jesus have used an argument of pragmatic utility to attract people into the community of faith? Did he not rather alert his generation to the cost of becoming his followers? Indeed he did, but we should not take that out of context. There is also a utilitarian side to Jesus and to the message of the Bible.

The book of Proverbs, for example, constantly asks us to consider wisdom which promises to make life good and valuable in the context of the fear of the Lord. Referring to wisdom, Proverbs says, "The man who finds me finds life, and the LORD will be pleased with him. The man who does not find me hurts himself; anyone who hates me loves death" (Proverbs 8:35-36). And Jesus too speaks of giving us "life in all its fullness" and promises that the person who gives his or her life over to him will find life (John 10:10; Mark 8:35). He said that discovering the message of the kingdom is like a merchant finding the pearl of great price which symbolizes the most valuable discovery a person could possibly make. I suggest that what he was getting at, at least in part, was the fact that his offer involved a new relationship with the gracious God which would satisfy our existential hungers and thirsts. It can open up for a person the possibility of solid meaning and significance so many people lack today. His message has obvious relevance to any reflective person who sees the need to establish his life on a firm foundation.

This book is concerned with verifying the truth of the gospel message. The sort of verification which circle one offers is pragmatic or experimental. It endeavors to point up the extreme relevance of the Christian message to our basic experience of living in the world. But what about the charge that this is all wishful thinking? Just because we feel the need for secure underpinnings beneath our lives does not establish that there are any.

I have two things to say to that. First, I don't think we can dismiss the significance of man's quest for meaning so easily. Surely the quest itself, revealing as it does a deep drive toward fulfillment, tells us something about ourselves and the world. I suppose it is possible to think that all it tells us is that the universe is a madhouse in which human creatures are born with deep desires incapable of fulfillment. "Too bad, but that's just the way it is!" But isn't it more sensible to say with C. S. Lewis,

"If I find in myself a desire which no experience in this world can satisfy, the most probable explanation is that I was made for another world"?[12] The Christian at any rate is not obliged to believe the depressing proposition that we are born with desires incapable of fulfillment, and the reader is not obliged to either.

Second, the person who objects that faith is wishful thinking needs to reckon on the equal possibility that atheism too may be the product of it. After all, one can also desire that God *not* exist so that he might not limit our autonomy or stand in the way of what we are planning to do. Because of our desire to do our own thing, we are often tempted to wish God out of existence. The objections cancel each other out.

At the same time I recognize that the Christian message cannot be completely established by the first circle alone but must be considered from other angles as well. Other evidences have to be placed alongside this circle to show that in addition to being relevant the gospel is also true in a factual sense. This leads us to consider circle two, the experiential basis for faith.

Chapter 2

Circle Two: The Experiential Basis for Faith

In circle one I have argued for the usefulness of faith on the basis of ordinary human experience. The biblical message supplies the necessary foundations for our confidence in the worth of human life. Alongside this evidence I now wish to place the data of religious experience. It would be no exaggeration to say that most men and women who come to faith, including the founders of great religions themselves, do so out of a profound experience of God's activity and presence in their lives. In the words of H. D. Lewis, "The core of religion is religious experience."[1]

A Remarkable Fact
In circle two I want to call the reader's attention to a most remarkable fact about the world we live in, but one we often disregard and take for granted, namely, the fact that enormous numbers of people have claimed to know God and to be

in contact with him. These are not just individuals from a certain stratum of society or from a certain limited set of human cultures, but include, as Elton Trueblood put it, "large numbers of those generally accounted the best and wisest of mankind."[2] The claim to be in contact with divine reality is so stupendous in itself and has been so regularly made that it cannot possibly be swept aside but must enter into any reasonable account of the nature of reality.

The advantage of this circle of evidence is surely obvious. Not only does it offer empirical evidence of the truth in addition to the pragmatic thrust of circle one but it offers evidence of a most important kind. Most people are not going to be content with the knowledge that faith is useful to them or that belief in God is rationally consistent with philosophical reflection, nor do they need to be. They will want to know God as a reality in their experience. Let's take an illustration from astronomy. In the past we often had to be satisfied with arguments that such and such a heavenly body must exist even though it could not be seen by the telescopes then available. But how much better it became when, by means of better equipment, we could actually focus our eyes on the planet in question. While it was perfectly valid to argue for the existence of the planet on the basis of inferences, seeing it directly with our own eyes is more convincing. After all, the strongest reason I have for believing in the moon is not the behavior of the ocean tides on earth, even though this corroborates that belief, but rather the sight of the moon shining in the dark night sky.

Take the famous case of Blaise Pascal. After his death a piece of paper was found sewn into the fabric of his coat describing a vivid encounter with God which took place in 1654 and gave direction to the last decade of his life (he died, aged thirty-nine). Dating his note November 23, 1654, he wrote, "From about half past ten in the evening to about half an hour after midnight, Fire."[3]

Thus he used but one word, *fire,* to describe what it was like, probably trying to bring out the indubitable quality we find in a flame which warms, lights and even burns. When we touch a flame we know we are not dreaming! It was an experience which flooded his soul with joy and light.

But by no means is all religious experience so dramatic, so transforming. At the other end of a spectrum is the quiet ordinary perception of the goodness and mystery of existence. In essence religious experience is rooted in a sense of *wonder* at the awesomeness of being which leaves us feeling dependent upon something unconditioned, something which is the source of all reality. Though by no means easy to define, and more intensely felt at some times than at others, it is a human experience widely attested and lying at the background of our lives most of the time. The uneducated as much as the enlightened find themselves vividly reminded of the limitations of their own existence and of their dependence upon a reality beyond themselves, mysterious and powerful. This awesome apprehension of the holy can come at times to vivid brilliant expression.

Unsecular Man
The evidence in circle two is not limited to the witness of religious people. It is far more extensive than overt expressions of religious experience. Even in secular writers who profess no faith it is common to discover close parallels in the form of the human passion to transcend oneself and the deep sense of cosmic contingency.

Although Jean Paul Sartre is an atheist, he finds it distressing that God does not exist because it leaves us stranded in space without a home or a goal to strive for. In striking words he stated, "God is silent and that I cannot possibly deny— everything in me calls for God and that I cannot forget. . . . As a matter of fact, this experience can be found in one form or another in most contemporary authors: it is the torment in

Jaspers, death in Malraux, destitution in Heidegger, the re-
prieved-being in Kafka, the insane and futile labour of Sisy-
phus in Camus."[4] Even in those who set their face against
God the awareness of Who is missing, as Sartre has noted, is
discernible.[5]

Ten years ago predictions were being made about the de-
cline of religion in secular society. Modern man was depicted
as one who had come of age and could easily dispense with
images of the sacred. The ensuing years have not borne out
these projections. Instead we have seen a revival of interest in
all manifestations of religion. We have seen a revolt against
one-dimensional man, the product of machine and computer,
and a continuing of the age-old quest for transcendence. The
older materialism simply does not satisfy, and people are
seeking God again.

The popularity of motion pictures like *Close Encounters of the
Third Kind* and *Star Wars* stems from the fact that they speak to
our cosmic loneliness. There really are gods in outer space
who are taking the initiative to make contact with us and make
themselves known to the young and the pure in heart. Clearly
these films express essentially religious themes, and people
are responding out of their very human hunger for worship.
They are feeling the truth of Jesus' words: "For what shall it
profit a man, if he shall gain the whole world and lose his own
soul?" (Mark 8:36 KJV).

Religion will persist into the future because it speaks to our
need to worship. Peter Schaffer brought this out clearly in
his play entitled *Equus.* In it he depicts a teen-aged boy who
has become attached to the symbol of Jesus in a picture on the
wall and an atheistic father who is determined to put an end to
such nonsense. In place of the picture of Jesus, the father
hangs the picture of a horse, hoping to divert his son's attention away from the one and onto the other. He is so successful that the boy begins to worship horses. Whereupon the
father sends him off to the psychiatrist to help the boy get rid

of the horse fixation. But this does not happen because the psychiatrist turns out to be jealous of the religious experience the boy enjoys in relation to it. He can see what joy it gave him and what a positive influence it was in his life. The boy had something to live for. How could he rob the patient of the worship which made him a more complete human being? The message that comes across is that worship defines a man, and the one who does not worship something greater than himself begins to shrink.[6]

The Lack of Universality
Although the number of those who have reported religious experiences is high, it does not include the entire human race. There are also fine people who frankly testify to the absence of any experience of God in their lives. What is the meaning of this negative evidence?

I believe we have to distinguish between the positive and negative evidence here. If someone sees a comet in the night and that is corroborated by a number of other viewers, the positive evidence stands and one begins to think about possible reasons everyone did not see it. Some were certainly asleep and so missed the sight. Others with weak vision did not notice anything different.

There are, in short, all kinds of reasons for the existence of negative evidence. People who have not yet encountered God should not conclude that those who have are misled but consider the possibility that there may be something to what they report.

The fact is that there are conditions underlying our experience of the world. I cannot see if I do not open my eyes. I cannot hear if my ears are plugged. It is no denial of the objectivity of sight or sound if we stress the importance of the receiving organ of sensation. The reality of God is not disproven just because it is not yet real to those who may not have met the conditions appropriate to knowing him.

And what might these be?

All religions emphasize the need to develop and mature in the spiritual disciplines that lead to the knowledge of God. In other words, the capacity and ability to know God, like the capacity to appreciate fine music, is a taste and awareness which needs to be exercised and nurtured. We would not think very much of a person who declared Bach to be a poor composer after only a half-hearted attempt to appreciate his music. So spiritual preparation is necessary for meaningful worship. If we are not open to God in a humble childlike way, for example, I don't think we can expect much reality should we encounter him. And if we are not willing to obey him when he reveals himself, I do not think we will ever really come to know him.

Of course, the awareness of the presence of God is not perfectly constant except in the lives of the most remarkable saints. Brother Lawrence may have been able to testify that he was never without a sense of God's presence, but many others have cried with the psalmist, "LORD, will you hide yourself forever?" (Psalms 89:46).

I certainly go through periods in my life when God seems distant from me or I from him, and I don't think this is always due to failure on my part. I think it relates to the sovereign freedom of God in giving himself to be known. The Spirit of God is like the wind that blows where it wills (John 3:8). It is not under our control.

Although there are steps toward spiritual preparation, they are not infallibly productive as if we could bend God to do our will. The knowledge of God is a gift and we cannot command it. Paradoxically at the same time it is God's standing offer: "The LORD says, 'Come, everyone who is thirsty —here is water! Come, you that have no money—buy grain and eat! Come! Buy wine and milk—it will cost you nothing!' " (Isaiah 55:1).

The Other Religions

Atheists have to believe all religions are false, and believers often believe they are all false but one. I do not think a Christian is forced to take such a narrow view. Paul explained that God never left himself without witness (Acts 14:17). He writes, "There is one God and Father of all mankind, who is Lord of all, works through all, and is in all" (Ephesians 4:6). Paul's glimpse of the universal sovereignty of God does not limit God's total activity to the knowledge of it we have been given in the Bible. C. S. Lewis says that he used to be troubled by the thought that salvation was confined to the people who had heard of Christ and were able to believe on him. It helped him to realize that "God has not told us what his arrangements about the other people are." He went on to comment, "In the meantime, if you are worried about the people outside, the most unreasonable thing you can do is to remain outside yourself."[7] I have been speaking about religious experience in general and not limiting my attention to Christian experience. How am I able to do so?

I think we should regard the great religions of the world as a patchwork quilt, combining light and dark colors in various proportions. All religions are not true in the same way. Their differences are deep-seated and cannot be smoothed over or disregarded. There are elements of truth and falsehood, authenticity and deception alongside each other in the fabric. There is a need for careful discernment.

But that is not to deny that in the world religions there are some good and positive features. There is devotion and commitment, often putting Christians to shame. The fundamental questions of life and death are also engaged there, and the quest for salvation pursued. In particular, there is the perception we are speaking of, some sense of the goodness and majesty of God and of our need to depend upon him in life and death. I believe God is dealing with everyone in the world even in the days of their searching before they come to explicit and settled faith, whether in the context of their religions or nonreligions. Any of their experiences can be used by God to bring them closer to knowing him.[8]

At the same time there are dark colors in the quilt too. Religion can also separate people from God and prevent them from meeting him. The religious of the world both image the real and also conceal it. But the positive witness is there.

Religious Experience and the Christian Message

Over and above the witness of religious experience in the universal context, I want to point to the centrality of it in the biblical faith. The prophets in the Old Testament regularly reported a conversion event when they personally encountered the powerful reality of God and surrendered their lives to his service. Paul's testimony was repeated three times in the book of Acts in order to authenticate the divine authority of his calling to proclaim the gospel. The experience of God's Spirit is one of the hallmarks of the Christian religion.

One way to highlight this dimension is to consider Jesus' experience of God. It is clear from the records of his life that his relationship with God his Father was warm and intimate. He depended upon prayer on a regular basis and especially in situations of crisis and decision. He knew God to be his Father in a special sense and himself to be the Father's Son in an intimate way. This assurance was fundamental to his mission. The experience, and not merely the intellectual conviction, of sonship sustained him throughout his career. He was conscious of having been commissioned by God to carry out a messianic mission, and he enjoyed a strong sense of authority as a result.

More than that, Jesus was conscious of the power of God's Spirit resting upon him. In the power of the Spirit he exercised his ministries of deliverance and healing. He was conscious of the power of God flowing through him and overcoming the powers of darkness, and claimed that it was evidence of the nearness of the longed-for kingdom of God in the presence of his hearers. The Spirit had indeed been poured out as the prophets had promised and the power of the kingdom was manifesting itself through him. His entire ministry reveals the conviction he expressed at the beginning of it: "The Spirit of the Lord is upon me" (Luke 4:18).[9]

The early Christians had the same experience. They testified to the reality of the Spirit of God poured out upon them. The church was born on the day of Pentecost in a communal experience of profound worship involving spiritual gifts and amid a sense of divine power uplifting and transforming them. The presence of God was almost tangible. Their meetings together were marked by exuberant joy and praise, a complete turnaround from the dark days after Jesus was put to death. More than a change in doctrinal convictions, what characterized this body of believers was the Spirit-filled nature of its common life and worship, its development and mission.

Of course there were dangers in a religion so oriented to spiritual experience, and Paul in particular had to face and deal with many of these. By calling attention to gospel truth, to love and the need for community upbuilding, he was able to check some of the disintegration latent in an enthusiastic movement like this. He knew that ecstatic phenomena occurred outside Christianity and were not in and of themselves distinctively Christian. Apart from certain safeguards they were ambiguous in value. Thus Paul was able to guide the church theologically in such a way that her life in the Spirit was a powerfully dynamic force rather than a divisive influence (1 Corinthians 12—14).

We can distinguish at least two modes of religious experience in the Christian life. First, there is what we could call the "charismatic" dimension in which the presence of God becomes almost unbearably real, including dramatic occasions in which the Lord seems to break into our ordinary lives in a crisis experience and in which very often the Spirit manifests himself in remarkable ways such as physical healing, prophecy and talking in tongues. It is God's way of reminding us that he is alive and active, willing to heal and save. Paul describes a situation in the church at Corinth where an unbeliever upon encountering God's powerful presence in the congregation found himself worshipping God and accepting the gospel message (1 Corinthians 14:25). Until this very day, and with special intensity in recent years, people have continued to witness to manifestations of power in the context of faith in Jesus.

Second, there is the experience of God's companionship in a quiet and regular way. Before his death Jesus promised to send the Paraclete or the Companion to be with us forever, a Friend that would never fail us. The Spirit would dwell within us and flow out from us like rivers of living water, he said. The Spirit would abide with us in every situation of life and never abandon us. His consoling and uplifting presence would give us joy and strength, drawing us up into fellowship with the Father and Jesus Christ his Son. Ordinary Christian experience involves a sense of loving care surrounding us and an encounter with the sacred revealed in Christ to be the living God, the Father of us all. In the fellowship of the church we celebrate the presence of the Lord and are renewed in strength as we wait upon him.

Religious experience is not the only circle of evidence available to confirm the truth claim of the gospel, but it is a very important one. There has been a tendency of late to interpret alienation from faith in intellectual rather than experiential terms. Academically oriented Christians especially tend to think that the barriers to faith should be removed by repackaging the content of the message in a way more congenial to the modern outlook. But it is quite possible that we are dealing, not so much with a failure of intellect, as with a failure of experience, an alienation from the experiential roots of Christianity itself so amply attested in the New Testament.

It may be then that the way to renewed commitment is less through intellectual and moral wisdom, though these are always needed, than by being drawn into the circle where you can taste and feel the love of the Lord in the company of those who know him. For many nothing will confirm the truth of the gospel like the personal encounter with God they crave. Apart from this experience all the other evidences we are discussing here tend to be abstract. Therefore we urge upon the reader openness to the initiatives of the Lord.

In Contrast to World-weariness

The point is this, those whose horizons are bounded by the material universe alone are often haunted by emptiness and a lack of direction. What is there to believe in and to hope for? Is not life a somewhat pointless business, offering little lasting satisfaction and fulfillment? In contrast, there stand the countless testimonies to the gracious presence of the Lord bringing strength and peace. As the angel said at the birth of Jesus, "I am here with good news for you, which will bring great joy to all the people" (Luke 2:10).

The Bible as well as Christian literature is full of witness to the peace and joy that comes from trusting God. He proves to be One who guides us and develops new resources in us to cope with the difficult situations of life. What we dimly sense is true: Life is not random and pointless, but providentially ordered on behalf of those who love the Lord. Each of our lives is unique and irreplaceable, and God has a plan and a purpose to pursue in each of them, if we open ourselves to him.

It has been so in my experience. The sweet savor of his presence has been real to me for over thirty years now, and the reliability of his companionship greater than that of any human friend. I can testify that God can be known and experienced as present, Spirit to spirit. The promises of God prove true to those who claim them. Therefore with the psalmist I make this appeal to my reader: "Find out for yourself how good the LORD is. Happy are those who find safety with him" (Psalms 34:8).

What Does It Prove?

The fact of religious experience must certainly be taken into account in any search for the meaning of life. But the question of its significance remains. A number of issues are involved.

First is the question of the amount and value of the evidence and the reliability of those reporting it. It is surely clear that the number of witnesses is extremely numerous, probably beyond counting. Some of them may have been deceived, but all of them? Even if only one of them is not deceived, the case is established. The quality of the evidence is also excellent, as good as in almost any field of inquiry.

The question, I think, boils down to this: Is our perceptual knowledge valid? If the weight of the evidence (a myriad of good reports from reliable witnesses) can be set aside, it is hard to see how we can avoid skepticism in the whole field of knowledge, something all of us wish to avoid. Setting aside so much high-quality evidence violates the mode by which we arrive at truth in all the other areas. We cannot reasonably sweep such testimony aside.

The evidence for the reality of God from religious experience is strong indeed. All of our beliefs, not only religious ones, are private in the sense that they are convictions of our minds, and all of them are rooted in the experience of ourselves and of others. Therefore the evidence here cannot be dismissed on the basis that it is inferior by reason of its subjectivity. Religious experience belongs to the entire sweep of human experience, and the evidence it presents is no better or worse than other kinds.

The second issue is the variety of religious experiences reported.[10] Such experiences range all the way from charismatic invasion to quieter impulses. Included, too, are the strange reports emanating from occult and psychic sources. What exactly do we know on the basis of religious experience? How much agreement is there in the reports?

Without wishing to deny considerable diversity in the reports, I wish to make a case for a good deal of convergence as well. Of course there are strange claims that are not easy to fit into any pattern, but there is also much agreement we should not disregard. Over and over again you get the feeling that you are hearing the same story of holiness, wonder and awe.

Think for a minute about how scientists disagree about their theories, and how science has changed radically over the past decades not to mention centuries. There is no greater diversity or change in religious experience than that! If we compare the science of two thousand years ago, for example, with the science of today, we find divergence at almost every point.

Such is *not* the case in religion. The history of science is the history of disagreements far more than is the history of religion. As Elton Trueblood put it, "The religion of a hundred years ago or of two thousand years ago does not seem quaint, for men can speak to each other about their knowledge of God, unhindered by the barriers of centuries."[11] How is it that we can sing the ancient psalms without feeling utterly anachronistic if not because the perception of God has remained essentially the same for three millennia? The corroboration of evidence from ancient times and widely separated cultures is uniquely impressive when compared with other fields of knowledge. Books in science are quickly out of date, but classics in religion are never out of date, because people today are compelled to agree with what they have perceived.

And what do they tend to agree about? They agree about the greatness and holiness of God who is absolute and compelling and demands our obedience. They agree about the unworthiness of man in the presence of God. They agree that behind this world of sense there lies a mystery toward which we ought to set our course, because it is a mystery that promises redemption to man. Although variety poses a problem in the area of religious experience, it is not an insuperable one and does not cancel the effectiveness of the witness to divine reality.

A third issue concerns the psychology of religion. It is still quite common to hear the charge that religious beliefs and experiences are little more than a projection of the human psyche conditioned by wishful thinking. But this objection cuts both ways. If belief in God can be a wish projection, the denial of God can be the product of wishful thinking too. Unbelief may also favor certain of our wishes, particularly the desire to be our own boss and run the whole show. The nonexistence of God can seem quite attractive to those who wish to live without regard to divine sovereignty. The fact that God meets certain human needs and wishes does not prove that he does not exist.

Psychological analysis of religious experience does, however, have some value. It is important to understand all we can about the processes of conversion and growth in faith. Without such study we may be unaware of forces which are really there. In particular it is important to expose religious belief which *is* just the result of psychological factors, for example, an immature refusal to accept responsibility. The Bible itself warns against spurious forms of faith and nominal forms of commitment which do not represent a serious decision for God but rather insulate a person from really meeting him.

What I do object to is a naturalistic reduction of the evidence of religious experience to the psychological plane. One's vision of the sunset is certainly related to the fact that he or she has eyes, but hardly limited to that fact. The existence of the sun has something to do with it too! Belief in God is certainly related to needs and aspirations which exist in the human heart, but that does not prove God himself is not the source of the experience. It is simply prejudice to debunk a whole mass of evidence on the basis of little more than the presupposition that there is no God.

More than that, it begs the question. Why infer God's *non*-existence from the existence of our need for God and religion? After all, most of our needs are capable of at least partial fulfillment. It would be a strange world indeed where the people in it required water and food and neither existed to fulfill their need. Yet that is the kind of world envisaged in this objection. We are being asked to believe that there is no fulfillment for our evident human need to transcend ourselves, that reality is mocking us at this point and that our basic religious need is one grand illusion.

I suggest that this view, while not unbelievable, is nevertheless incredible. It is easier to believe it at the top of our heads than in the bottom of our hearts. I urge the reader who has not yet found God to continue the search and not conclude he does not exist just because we need him to exist. Consider instead the possibility that you have not yet looked in the right place. Hear the words of Jesus, "Come to me, all of you who are tired from carrying heavy loads, and I will give you rest" (Matthew 11:28). A relationship with him is not an illusion born out of your desire to know God; it is the fulfillment of that fundamental need.

Religious experience tells us something important about ourselves. It uncovers our deep desire to find fulfillment in a realm beyond the material. It is a basic human intuition which stands as proof of the reality of the spiritual. Though it could be a quirk in human development that mocks him, surely it is more likely firm evidence that we are spiritual beings, and that God exists and is willing to be known. I take this dimension of experience to be an important clue to the nature of reality and place it alongside the other circles of credibility as a standing witness.

Christian Hedonism?

At the end of two circles I find myself in an embarrassing position. As I look back over the two arguments I see that I have presented the Christian message as the fulfillment of two basic human drives: the drive toward meaning and the drive toward transcendence. I have seen the gospel as making us happy and fulfilling our needs, as giving us pleasure and satisfaction.

But is this right? What about the strong conviction many have that the Christian life ought to be difficult and painful, that it should mean being deprived and going without things? Is holiness really fun?

Yes, I think it is. Though it is true that following Christ in this world the way it is will involve tension and pain, it is also true that following him guarantees us infinite joy and fullness of life. Jesus himself said, "I have come in order that you might have life, life in all its fullness" (John 10:10). The Christian way is not hedonism in the ordinary sense, of course. It does not make a god out of sensual pleasure. But it does involve enjoying God and his gifts, pleasure deeper than all others. Let me close with the psalmist again:

Seek your happiness in the LORD,
    and he will give you your heart's desire.
Give yourself to the LORD;
    trust in him, and he will help you. (Psalm 37:4-5)

How precious, O God, is your constant love!
    We find protection under the shadow of your wings.
We feast on the abundant food you provide;
    you let us drink from the river of your goodness.
You are the source of all life,
    and because of your light we see the light. (Psalm 36:7-9)
God according to the Christian message is no killjoy!

Chapter 3

Circle Three: The Cosmic Basis for Faith

So far I have been dealing in existential matters, looking at dimensions of human experience. It is important, I think, to demonstrate the relevance of the gospel to the lived-out character of our human existence. The Christian faith supplies the needed foundation of meaning and the longed-for fountain of living water that can satisfy our spiritual thirsts. If it couldn't do those things, it would hardly deserve a second glance. But since it can, there is reason to go further into other evidence for its truth.

Circles three and four present evidence more strictly intellectual than existential. Faith has to be thought through as well as lived out, and so it is important to subject its claims to the test of critical thought. Man is a thinking as well as a feeling creature, and we must reflect on the philosophical and historical credentials of the Christian message. Such reflection ought to highlight more precisely the objective and even factual truth of the gospel in a way the first circles can not. To change the image, there is soft (existential) evidence and hard (factual) evidence to deal with; both are important in the total evidential picture.

Natural Theology: The Proclamation of the Skies

When I speak of the cosmic basis for faith, I am referring to the witness to the reality of God which I believe is displayed in the universe itself by virtue of its having been created by God. I hold with John Calvin that,

> There are innumerable evidences both in heaven and on earth that declare His wonderful wisdom; not only those more recondite matters for the closer observation of which astronomy, medicine, and all natural science are intended, but also those which thrust themselves upon the sight of even the most untutored and ignorant persons, so that they cannot open their eyes without being compelled to witness them.[1]

Calvin's point is supported in the Bible, even though it like Calvin devotes far more space to the declaration of the mighty acts of God and their theological significance, the subject of circle four. The psalmist declares, "How clearly the sky reveals God's glory! How plainly it shows what he has done!" (Psalms 19:1). The apostle Paul taught that every human being—all of us—possesses sufficient knowledge of the truth about God to render us without excuse for not worshiping or feeling grateful to him. God's reality is displayed all around us in the creation, and we cannot help but see it. He writes, "Ever since God created the world, his invisible qualities, both his eternal power and his divine nature, have been clearly seen; they are perceived in the things that God has made" (Romans 1:19). The world itself is a standing witness to the fact that God is its creator.

There are many other precedents in the Old Testament to back up what Paul wrote too. The first chapter of Genesis brings out a vivid sense of the wisdom and intelligence of God in creating the world to be inhabited by man. As Isaiah the prophet puts it, "He formed and made the earth—he made it firm and lasting. He did not make it a desolate waste, but a place for people to live" (45:18). The Hebrews had a profound sense of the symmetry and teleology inhering in the universe, created as it was by the wisdom and knowledge of the Lord (Proverbs 3:19-20). It caused another psalmist to cry out, "LORD, you have made so many things! How wisely you made them all! The earth is filled with your creatures" (Psalms 104:24).[2]

There is undoubtedly a mystery about the universe which baffles the human mind and inclines it upon the quest of understanding and explanation. Before the rise of secular patterns of thought most people looked toward religion to give them some hint of the meaning of the totality of existence. By means of its myths and symbols, religion has long sought to supply answers to these deeply philosophical questions.

In the context of Greek philosophy, however, the science of *metaphysics* also developed. Metaphysics involves rational reflection on being and its ultimate significance. Rooted in a sense of wonder (why are things as they are?), metaphysics is the rather audacious attempt to comprehend the meaning of the world as a whole and come to some conclusion about its purpose. It is the philosophical equivalent to the drive toward meaning we discussed in the first circle.

There was a time, in the Middle Ages, when most Christian thinkers believed it was possible to demonstrate by strict argument that God exists.[3] Elements in Greek philosophy were appropriated and combined with biblical ideas to form the classical theistic arguments such as Thomas Aquinas promulgated. But along came modern philosophy, bringing with it trenchant criticisms of these "proofs" which showed them to be defective in various ways. As a result philosophy and theology turned away from metaphysics, or natural theology as it came to be called, and began to focus on religious experience and morality.

Some of the criticisms were well taken. For example, it was arrogant to claim certainty for these arguments. The criticisms have thus had the good effect of humbling the natural theologians and making them more modest. Furthermore, the categories in which the classical proofs were formulated are not modern and do not sound persuasive to most people today. At the same time, a gap still remains between theistic belief and rational reflection on the world, and it still needs to be bridged. New styles of natural theology I think are well fitted for this task. The purpose of this effort is not to erect abstract, watertight proofs for the existence of God, but rather to connect sound thinking about the world on the one hand with the Christian belief in God on the other. I personally think that the prospects of doing this are brighter now than they have been for some time.

The reason such an exercise as natural theology exists is the wonder-evoking quality of existence in the world. How did the world come to be? Why does it exist? And what is man's place in it? It is not easy to shake these questions off once they have been raised.

Our course is set to discover, if we can, the ultimate explanation of things. It is man's nature to want to find out. We are teleological beings, set upon finding clues to the meaning of it all. Camus spoke of it as the "wild longing for clarity whose call echoes in the human heart."

It is my contention that the universe raises the question of God in a number of ways and that belief in God makes the best rational sense and has more explanatory power in accounting for it than any alternative. In particular it seems to me that the humanist solution, that matter itself is the sole originating cause of the world, requires far more faith than the Christian message does.[4]

The Marvels of Design

In a world so influenced and impressed by scientific reasoning as ours is, it is inevitable that one argument which will seem plausible and relevant intellectually will have a scientific cast to it. Being intrigued at the way things are composed and how they work, our minds are open to the argument for God's existence based on the high degree of design which is manifested in the world.

Consider the human brain, for example. It consists of about three pounds of grey matter, and yet no manmade computer of any size can duplicate the myriad of operations it routinely performs for us every day. Composed of thirty billion nerve cells, the brain is a vast, largely unexplored continent—one of the wonders of the universe. How can a person be expected to believe that an organ of such incredible complexity and versatility came to exist by accident as the result of an unintelligent and purely material process?

And then there is the matter of the thinking activity which the brain sustains. Is it reasonable to think that this eruption of intelligence burst forth in a world in essence mindless? Indeed, why would we take reasoning seriously at all if the thought processes themselves are really only material interactions? The mind in a mindless universe is a contradiction, an anomaly, but it is not at all surprising if the universe is as theists understand it. Brains and minds in a world created by pure Intelligence—that is what one would expect.

Besides the brain, of course, there are dozens of other marvels contained in the biology of a human being. Often and justly referred to is the amazing performance of the eye and the electrochemical operations it performs to give us instantaneous color vision. Unless a person chooses to be willfully ignorant, it is impossible not to be startled by the amazing complexity involved. The same is true of the ear and hearing, the blood, the heart, the kidneys and what we call the "simple cell." Each one of the sixty trillion cells in our body performs a series of operations and is a storehouse of information.

How is it possible that such order and design has come about by random selection apart from the supervision of divine intelligence? Once such organs had arrived on the scene, there would be no difficulty understanding why they would survive. The creature with excellent sight would win out over one without it, other things being equal. It is the *arrival* and not the survival of them that amazes me. The problem is to account for the remarkable process which throws up these marvels in the first place.

This is particularly true in the case of complex organs whose ability to function and thus contribute to their own survival value depends on their being in a state of near perfection. An organ like the eye can hardly prove its worth until a whole set of interlocking preconditions is in place. This has caused some biologists to suggest a theory of macromutations, since a long series of micromutations will not provide the explanation for it. In other words, a scientific version of a miracle is required to make sense of what we observe.

I am arguing that things appear to be purposefully arranged. The adaptive harmony we see in the world is meant to be a signal to us about the existence of a Creator. If we saw a scattering of stones on a hillside spelling out the words, "Welcome to Canada," we would not suppose that these stones had fallen down the hill and formed the message by themselves. They could have done so, but it would be very unlikely. Instead we would conclude that some intelligent agent had arranged the stones in that pattern so as to communicate with us. I believe it is reasonable to think that God wants to communicate with us and does so in part through the wise ordering of the world, which is a cosmos not a chaos.

Believing in the existence of God is something like believing in a scientific theory. Even though it cannot be directly tested, as many scientific theories cannot be, there is a lot of data which indirectly confirms it. It makes sense out of a whole host of facts. By contrast, the idea that matter evolving blindly, without purpose, has produced all that we now see is implausible. How could it possibly do so? Belief in God, on the other hand, puts the mind at rest when it comes to contemplating these things.

The Creation of the World

On a wider angle still, people have been astonished at the bare existence of the universe. Why is there something rather than nothing? Is there a sufficient reason to account for the existence of the world? In philosophical circles the debate goes round and round between those who contend that a finite universe must needs be in a state of dependency upon an infinite Being which is unlimited. The general public is not in a position to judge the merits of either side adequately, and the experts are badly divided. For me the argument has an anachronistic ring to it and is difficult to formulate in a way that seems convincing.

But there is another form of the argument which is easy to state and seems very convincing, revealing again our preference for proofs which are scientific in form. It relates to the discovery that the universe had its beginning a long time ago in a gigantic explosion that some call the "act of creation." According to some first-class astronomers, the first verse of the Bible has come into high repute: "In the beginning God created the heavens and the earth" (RSV). Writing in the *New York Times*, Robert Jastrow, director of NASA's Goddard Institute for Space Studies and author of many scholarly studies in astronomy, asks the question, "Have Astronomers Found God?" and considers it very likely that they have, or come close to it.[5] His investigations have led him to conclude that the universe had a beginning at a certain moment in time, and although science cannot itself prove it came into being by an act of God, that explanation is a reasonable possibility.

"Now we see how the astronomical evidence leads to a biblical view of the origin of the world," he writes. "The details differ, but the essential elements in the astronomical and biblical accounts of Genesis are the same: the chain of events leading to man commenced suddenly and sharply at a definite moment in time, in a flash of light and energy." His closing words are remarkable:

> This is an exceedingly strange development, unexpected by all but the theologians. They have always believed the word of the Bible. But we scientists did not expect to find evidence for an abrupt beginning because we have had until recently such extraordinary success in tracing the chain of cause and effect backward in time. . . . At this moment it seems as though science will never be able to raise the curtain on the mystery of creation. For the scientist who has lived by his faith in the power of reason, the story ends like a bad dream. He has scaled the mountains of ignorance; he is about to conquer the highest peak; as he pulls himself over the final rock, he is greeted by a band of theologians who have been sitting there for centuries.

Jastrow is aware of the resistance to his theory on the part of fellow scientists, not on the basis of contrary evidence so much as from antireligious prejudice. It upsets them to think that science might actually turn up evidence against the naturalistic presumption upon which so much recent science is based. It would make it no longer possible to exclude God *a priori* even in scientific work.

Dr. Jastrow, though not a believer himself, has put his finger on the ultimately religious presuppositions that play an important role in all human thought. His work also touches on moral issues, for it compels those who find the possibility of creation repugnant, as many do, to ask themselves why they do so. Is it because they cannot bear to think that the entire enterprise of life and existence is not autonomous and self-explanatory or that there is a limit to what their minds can describe and conclude? It is exciting to think that the lines of communication between religion and science might be open again after a century when the dialog had been largely broken off. What we have to face up to is that the new cosmology sounds very much like the story the Bible has been telling us all along: "It is by faith that we understand that the universe was created by God's word" (Hebrews 11:3).

I do not think we can demonstrate conclusively that the world was created by God rather than having existed forever on its own. But that does not put an end to the question. Suppose that you came upon a large glass ball on a forest path while you were out for a walk. It attracted your attention, and made you wonder why it was there and how it got there. It would be possible just to conclude it had always been there. Even though its presence on the path may indeed be a gratuitous fact with no explanation, I doubt that anyone would be satisfied with such an answer.

Why not? Because there is within us a drive to understand which will not easily accept being put off like that. We feel cheated intellectually when we are told something has no explanation. When we spend our lives searching for intelligible understanding in all areas, we do not like to be told in the case of the universe that it has no explanation, when it obviously needs one. It goes against the principle of rationality all of us have been operating on till now.

If reality is ultimately absurd and inexplicable, why should we live as if it were not so? Small wonder, if philosophy or science contend there is no ultimate explanation for the existence of the world, that artists and writers conclude there is no meaning at other levels either. Or conversely, the argument of circle one about the need for faith to satisfy the drive toward existential meaning rests upon the strong metaphysical conviction that the existence of an intelligent Creator makes better sense of the universe than eternal mindless matter does.

Our lives are characterized by the desire to know and understand, and the context in which this drive makes fullest sense is the world as it is understood in the Christian message.[6] According to secularism, our minds and our whole beings are fragile sparks cast up into the darkness of unreason by an accidental collocation of atoms and they are destined to be snuffed out by the ongoing clash of material forces.

This image may be the boldest myth ever projected in the history of culture. For sheer drama and pathos it surpasses in scope and intensity the tales of Greece and Norway. But how can it be true? It asks us to believe that the very powers of reason we are here employing based on our intense desire to know are nothing more than the "unforeseen and unintended by-product of a mindless process at one stage of its endless and aimless becoming."[7]

The content of the myth knocks out from under us the ground for believing it to be true! And it suggests that human nature's drive to understand itself tells us nothing about the nature of reality. Without God I believe the intelligibility of the universe is foreclosed and our drive to understand a mere mockery.

A Dozen Other Clues

One reason natural theology has gotten a bad name for itself is that people have received the impression that its arguments are all of a difficult philosophical nature. Little has been done to correct this impression. But, as a matter of fact, the witness of creation to the reality of God is far richer and more diverse than that.

Take the experience of beauty for example. In our appreciation of works of art and music we are all familiar with a form of communication which comes to us from the artist or composer. The craftsman has introduced into his or her medium elements of creative design which we are able to detect and interpret. We know that we are not in the presence of accident and chance (normally!) but are experiencing intelligence, thought and feeling through interacting with the work.

Do we not often have the same experience in encountering the physical universe as well? Here too we are impressed with the world as a work of art and feel drawn to express gratitude to the unseen Artist. Indeed, upon further reflection are we not also led to feel that the capacity in us to appreciate beauty (which from a secular standpoint must seem an unaccounted-for "extra" thrown in by chance) is the finite reflection of the supreme Craftsman, the Maker of all things? Otherwise the capacity seems inexplicable, lacking as it does any survival value in terms of our evolution.

Consider too the "problem" of pleasure. Yes, I mean the problem of pleasure, not the problem of pain about which we hear so much more. It is another example of things we take so much for granted but which, if we think on it, are clues to the nature of reality. Of course pleasure and pain do possess considerable survival value. Pain warns us away from hurtful and harmful sensations, and pleasure encourages us to eat and reproduce ourselves. But there seems to be a surfeit of pleasure beyond what is strictly needed for that, as if the Maker wanted to see us glad.

It is true, of course, that many do not enjoy a great deal of satisfaction in this life, and none of us experiences the perfect delight we crave. There always seems to be a falling off of pleasure which makes us long for more. These things are significant from the Christian standpoint which sees human destiny in terms of perfect fulfillment in a relationship with God that lasts forever. We were created for pleasure and happiness, and that is what we can enjoy. As the psalmist puts it, "In thy right hand are pleasures for evermore" (Psalm 16:11 RSV). Perfect joy is held out to the one who receives the desire of the nations, the Messiah, Jesus.

There are many other clues too in our personal life. Basic to our self-understanding is our openness to the world, our restlessness to press on beyond the limits of the present and strive for the goals that lie out in front of us. We understand ourselves to be personal agents, able in our finite freedom to shape a future for ourselves and to go beyond the structured world to create that which is really new. Of course our freedom is not unlimited. We cannot achieve full mastery over the world. But we can and do strive to arrange the world in a better way, and we treasure hope for unlimited fulfillment.

It seems to me that this view of human nature which we as modern people have is close to the biblical understanding. God made us to be a creature like himself, open to the world, a history maker. God himself is the goal for which we strive ultimately and the rock on which we in our finitude are forced to depend. He is also the foundation of our hope for the future, the "God of hope" (Romans 15:13 RSV).

But what if there is no such God? How then shall we understand ourselves? It does not make much sense to think a blind process of chance threw up such semi-transcendent beings as we are. I suppose that explains why there are psychologists like B. F. Skinner committed to proving we are wrong to think of ourselves as personal agents at all. Surely the intuition of our personal freedom sits more securely within a theistic than within a nontheistic understanding of the world. Man is personal because reality is personal at its root and core. In the world which the Christian message presupposes, the personhood of human beings is not an embarrassment but a triumph.[8]

The Moral Dimension

I have already referred to the moral dimension of human experience in circle one. I suggested there that foundational to morality was a confidence in the worthwhileness of life which betokens belief in God as its only sufficient basis. But there are several other aspects to morality which raise the question of God as well.

One was noted by Immanuel Kant in the *Critique of Practical Reason,* in which he explained why God needed to be postulated to make sense of moral experience. The argument goes like this. In this life goodness is not always accompanied by happiness but it ought to be. Morality is in an unfinished state as far as this world is concerned. If this is to be corrected, we are compelled to postulate both God and immortality so that by his power the defect will be corrected and the environment for moral fulfillment provided.

The heart of Kant's argument is the sense of incongruity he feels with the secular account of morality; it leaves our sense of morality frustrated and short of its proper goal. The denial of God and immortality means that we whose lives are oriented toward moral goodness and beatitude but fall short of realizing them are forever denied the end for which we long. This is not the case with human drives in general, and I do not believe it is so here either. Humanism would mean that we human beings are the one organism not granted the conditions appropriate to our latent powers. The grandeur of man, in this case his moral inclinations, turns out to be his misery and frustration. The Christian message does not see it so.

One other aspect of morality worth noting is the sense of duty and obligation we often feel, an imperative above and beyond the demands of expediency and self-interest. Humanism tends to consider moral norms to be a matter of personal opinion and taste. But the moral conscience often leads us further than that. In the trials of Nazi war criminals, for example, few people took the view that what a man like Eichmann did was justified because these acts were acceptable according to the criteria he himself recognized. Most felt, and this is why he was condemned and executed, that genocide was absolutely and objectively evil and those who practice it deserve to die. Humanism can judge actions morally unpleasant, but has difficulty judging them morally wrong, as our moral experience often requires.

The idea we all admire—that the neighbor as a person has an absolute claim upon us and cannot be reduced to the means to an end—makes most sense on a religious basis. The moral imperative is an expression of belief in a moral God who rules the universe in a moral fashion. The worth of other people is guaranteed by the fact that they are created, loved and destined for eternal life with him. The value we attach to them is the value bestowed upon them by God. Our sense of moral responsibility is rooted in our actual personal responsibility to an infinite, personal God. The sense of guilt we feel when we fall short of the moral good is the feeling of betraying the One whose law upholds the universe. In so many ways the existence of God makes sense out of the moral life.[9]

The Quest for Intelligibility

For me belief in God is the end of my quest for intelligibility. It is not only an existential matter but a rational conviction as well. I am well aware of the limits of human reason and how relative the arguments of natural theology are to the epochs in which they were first developed. But at the same time it is important for each generation to try to make sense of the world, to try to gain a coordinated vision of reality, to decide about the meaning and significance of the whole. My aim has been to present some of the factors which impress me with the ultimate intelligibility of the whole on the basis of belief in God.

A stream does not rise higher than its source. It is not reasonable to believe that there are effects such as personality, morality, freedom and intelligence in the world which were not present in the cause of it. It simply does not make full sense to suppose that matter, mindless, amoral and impersonal, is the sole originating cause of things. Perhaps I could believe it if I did not think very much about it. But as it is, the proposal seems incredible.

I know it sounds a little strange for a man of faith to be

complaining that secular beliefs require too much faith to be accepted. But that is the way it is. Humanism, though easy to accept because it is the cultural myth and the accepted religion of the modern intelligentsia, is in actual fact impossible to believe because it stretches credulity beyond the breaking point. It is theistic belief that makes sense of the world. Atheism is just too hard to accept.

I am not suggesting for a moment that belief in God is usually created by a process of reasoning such as this, or that a person who has not seen some proof for God cannot know God. Certainly not. I have already argued that some knowledge of God is given along with ordinary human experience as we go about our ordinary activities, and some is communicated in the form of religious experience itself.

The arguments I have been discussing here reflect a deeper awareness of God which in fact underlies this effort. These arguments are an attempt to elaborate that more fundamental and original knowledge which is accessible to everyone. This is why some are helped by the arguments, while others can do perfectly well without them. The proofs do not communicate a knowledge otherwise unknown, as if God were a subject some did not happen to notice until they saw him at the end of an argument. No, the reason for arguments like these is the desire to test rationally what we already suspect and are concerned about. As Karl Rahner puts it, "A theoretical proof for the existence of God is only intended to mediate a reflexive awareness of the fact that man always and inevitably has to do with God in his intellectual and spiritual existence, whether he reflects upon it or not, and whether he freely accepts it or not."[10]

From one standpoint this relativizes the importance of theistic arguments. But from another standpoint it places the effort in the proper context, which is to test belief in God from the point of view of its rationality. There is, after all, value in clarifying even beliefs which are implicit and primordial.

A Steppingstone

In his mission to Lystra the apostle Paul recognized the revelation of God to the people of Asia Minor and used it as a steppingstone to proclaim the good news of Jesus to them. From the earlier disclosure alone they were not in a position to have very much specific information about the God who loved them. It is the same with these arguments here. While they incline our minds to consider a God who is moral, personal, powerful, intelligent and the like, they do not preach the good news of God as Redeemer and Father to us. They lead us to consider sympathetically that proclamation in the next circle but they do not make it themselves.

As soon as we are alert to the possibility of God's existence, the great question becomes what God is like. Indeed for most people that may well be the most important question. They do not need proof that God exists so much as clarity as to what he is like. This is why the message of the Incarnation stands at the heart of the Christian gospel. Through that event we learn of the graciousness of God and of his plan to save mankind in a way we find nowhere else. Natural theology is not an end in itself, but a *preparatory step* in the direction of taking that message seriously.

This same point bears upon the weakness that has always dogged the steps of natural theology, the problem of evil. The world is fallen and suffering, and does not provide us with a true reflection of reality as it was originally intended. Because of evil some have even concluded that God, if indeed he exists, must either be incompetent or evil himself. Although there are things that can be said to refute such a dire conclusion, there is nothing better than the gospel itself which is fundamentally God's answer to the problem of evil. Apart from the biblical message much in the world remains dark and mysterious, but in the light of it we receive confidence and hope again.

God is not aloof and indifferent to our condition, but is One who hears our cry and suffers with us and for us. Nothing in natural theology can tell us that. All it can do is propel us forward to enquire after the historical credentials of the good news about Jesus who proclaims God with a human face.

Chapter 4

Circle Four:
The Historical
Basis
for Faith

*pragmatic
experience
cosmic*

The purpose of the three circles so far discussed is to establish the general cogency of the theistic world view presupposed in the Christian message. They establish the background against which the claim to revelation made for the preaching about Jesus Christ can be weighed and understood. If there were no reason to think in terms of the existence of God, then the message of and about Jesus would have little force. As it is, I think we are ready to ask if there is any solid historical evidence for supposing as Christians do that Jesus is the light of the world because he is the incarnate Son of the Father. The first three circles raise the question we need to face, Has there been a decisive self-disclosure of God in human history?

Religion for the Tough-minded
Tough-minded people, according to William James, are those

who have a great respect for facts and do not respond to appeals to their emotional side. Although people of that sort often keep away from religion because so much of it deals in tenderhearted concerns, they ought to give the Christian message close attention because it by contrast puts a lot of weight on the factual character of its central theme. It even welcomes those who wish to scrutinize and criticize it, confident that it can pass any fair test.

The gospel in essence is a newscast. It concentrates its attention upon what God has done in history for the salvation of mankind. That is why it contains little of what we have called natural theology. It is not that the Bible is against sincere efforts to make sense of belief in God in terms of his revelation in nature and the world, but that it is so much more interested in God's revelation in human history. The fullness of truth is revealed according to Hebrew thinking through what *happens* rather than what *is*, and this explains the emphasis. — communication

The Bible claims that God has revealed himself decisively in historical events. At the heart of Israel's faith in the Old Testament was the grateful remembrance of how God delivered them from bondage in Egypt and how he led them to a new homeland. The gospel in the New Testament focuses on a greater deliverance from a deeper bondage, the redemption of humanity from sin through the person and work of Jesus.

Christians believe that the eternal Word of God became flesh in time-space history and that, after a public ministry of announcing God's coming kingdom and its righteousness, and suffering death on the cross for the sake of sinners, God the Father vindicated Jesus by raising him from the dead and making him Lord of all. We believe this to be a fact capable of being tested and verified. We do not see it as an occult truth vouchsafed only to the initiated few, but an objective act of God in history which confronts all mankind with its force.

I do not expect you as readers to have faith before examining the claims for Jesus, but only to approach the subject with an open mind, be willing to take the data seriously and be open to its implications. I am personally convinced that there is good evidence that the message about Jesus is true, that it is not merely the result of wishful thinking. In that spirit I want to lay out some of the evidence.

According to the biblical outlook the revelation of God in Jesus anticipates the consummation of the kingdom which is still awaited when "all mankind" shall see "the glory of the LORD" (Isaiah 40:5). One day the curtain which conceals the mystery of God's dealings with mankind will be drawn back. Then the ways of God will be totally vindicated and clarified in an irresistible fashion. Before this happens there will be some questions that go unanswered and much that remains unresolved. What the gospel announces in the meantime is that the clue to the mystery of human history and the secret of God's plan to bring all things to their purposed goal is Jesus Christ himself. By placing oneself in relation to Christ by faith, a person is caught up in the saving process.

The Fact of Christ

The center of the New Testament is Jesus Christ. Therefore my central concern in seeking to commend the reasonableness of faith is to expose to view the person of Jesus Christ who ministered, lived and died, and who was raised from the dead by the Father to be the Lord of the universe and Savior of the world.[1] Therefore the credibility of this conviction will be the substance of my remarks in circle four. Everything else would seem to hang upon it. As Paul said, "If Christ has not been raised from death, then we have nothing to preach and you have nothing to believe" (1 Corinthians 15:14). I will proceed on the assumption that Paul was right in his remarkably tough-minded assertion. The converse, of course, is also true: if he has been raised, we all ought to be prepared to commit ourselves to him.

Since our access to Jesus must be through the primary historical sources we call Gospels, I had better begin by discussing the reliability of those documents. Although doubt is often expressed about their authenticity, I fail to see any objective basis for taking a skeptical attitude.

One such skeptic is Rudolf Augstein, the publisher of *Der Spiegel,* West Germany's best-known news weekly, who argues that the picture of Jesus presented in the Gospels is the product of the church's creative imagination.[2] Ironically he depends for much of his case upon critics of the text like Rudolf Bultmann who do not intend to destroy faith in Christ by their criticism as Augstein does. In any case the attempt fails because it ignores the credentials of authenticity the Gospels display.

For one thing the early dating of the New Testament documents does not support the theory that legends grew up around the figure of Jesus in the absence of historical controls. Paul's letters are firmly dated in the first decades after the death of Christ, and he refers to the eyewitnesses that he knew and talked with. Mark wrote his Gospel a mere thirty years after Jesus died; he designed it for Christians in Rome who were suffering under Nero's persecution of them.

Thirty years is *not* a very long time. Imagine a person writing today about the second world war and dreaming up all kinds of events that never happened. He wouldn't get away with it because there are so many around who can still remember those days as if they were yesterday. But it is the same short period we are talking about in the case of Mark's Gospel. In an important recent study J. A. T. Robinson argues that every one of the twenty-seven New Testament books was written before A.D. 70.[3] Whether or not he is correct, it is still true that there is not enough time to make Augstein's theory plausible.

Consider, too, the Aramaic idiom in which the sayings of

Jesus exist in the Gospels. The way Jesus spoke, the terms he used, the parallelism and rhythm of his speech all confirm that the material goes back to the Palestinian setting of Jesus' life and do not derive from the Hellenistic context of the churches later on. What we are hearing in the Gospels is the voice of Jesus himself.

Concerning this and after a full presentation of this evidence Professor Joachim Jeremias comments, "The linguistic and stylistic evidence shows so much faithfulness and such respect towards the tradition of the sayings of Jesus that we are justified in drawing up the following principle of method: in the synoptic tradition it is the inauthenticity, and not the authenticity, of the sayings of Jesus that must be demonstrated."[4]

In an interesting study of Roman law as it appears in the Gospels and Acts in the proceedings against Jesus and Paul, A. N. Sherwin-White provides a similar case of verification in favor of the Gospels. It seems that the legal details mentioned in the trial narratives of the Gospels correspond exactly with what we know of Roman practice during the first half of the first century A.D. Had the writers not been in touch with the facts they could not have gotten the procedures right because of the variations that were introduced into them by the time they actually wrote. Sherwin-White's book ends with a strong plea for fairness in evaluating the Gospels which as historically reliable sources, he feels, compare favorably with the best in the field of classical studies. He expresses surprise and dismay at the tendency displayed by Augstein and others who should know better than to downgrade the historicity of the New Testament sources despite such strong objective evidence in their favor.[5]

Some people's doubt about the historical value of the Gospels seems to be a combination of dubious critical methods mixed with unbelief in the story they relate. As to method some critics insist on asking the negative question, Why should we accept such and such a saying on Jesus' lips when it could have been said by someone else? When one approaches historical sources in that way, very little that is positive emerges. A skeptical conclusion is almost assumed in the question. One is predisposed to a negative result.

Often along with this attitude something called the principle of dissimilarity is used too. This principle assumes that nothing should be considered authentic if it is paralleled either in rabbinic sources or in the thought of the early church. That means, in practice, that Jesus' voice can only be heard when he goes against the Hebrew tradition and also the thought of his own followers. So limited a criterion must necessarily create a distorted effect. Undoubtedly what survives such criticism must necessarily be authentic, but there is no excuse for setting the hurdle so high.

On the other hand, the principle yields some important evidence on behalf of the genuineness of the material. In the Gospels Jesus engages in controversy over sabbath observance, which was not a major issue in the early church, and does not say anything about the practice of circumcision, which was an issue. This surely indicates that the Gospels are reporting what Jesus did and did not teach and not placing on his lips matters of interest to them at a later date. Paul respected historical accuracy too when he distinguished between the words which the Lord Jesus spoke while on earth and what he himself thought about a certain matter (1 Corinthians 7:10, 12). Obviously it was not his custom to attribute to Jesus words he did not actually speak even though some prophet may have pronounced them or Paul himself thought them infallibly true.

In summary, the historical quality of the New Testament sources justifies an open disposition toward what they report and excludes a skeptical approach. I am not asking anyone to accept the text uncritically, but only to give it a fair hearing which the facts demand.

Who Then Was Jesus?

Jesus was first of all a preacher of good news about the kingdom of God. In summary his message was, "The right time
has come . . . and the Kingdom of God is near! Turn away
from your sins and believe the Good News!" (Mark 1:15). The
kingdom of God denotes the manifest rule of God whose intervention will bring history to its appointed end in salvation and
judgment. Since it is the next event mankind will face from
God's hand, they are urged to make a decision in relation to it.
At that time God's kingdom was manifesting itself through
the words and actions of Jesus himself. The long-cherished
messianic age was beginning to dawn, and the kingdom was in
the midst of his hearers in a preliminary way (Luke 17:20-21).

The most important feature of this present opportunity for
mankind according to Jesus was the generosity of God who
desires to entertain all who will come to the great feast of salvation (Matthew 8:11; 22:9-10). Although people are sinners
and owe God a great debt metaphorically speaking, Jesus said
God would cancel their debt and receive them into fellowship
with him by grace through faith. Jesus preached the merciful
pardon of God to all including the greatest of sinners, and he
urged his hearers to accept the grace of God and to show they
had accepted it by living lives of grace and mercy in response.

Good News

He compared accepting God's offer of salvation to finding
the pearl of great price, something so valuable that one sells
everything else to obtain it (Matthew 13:45-46). According to
the gospel, the God of the universe is in love with us and desires our fellowship in an everlasting covenant. He is asking us
to decide now whether we will enter into this relationship,
whether we will seize upon the opportunity or let it slide by.

In addition to preaching, Jesus acted in a way that reflected
his own words. He did not belong to the religious or political
establishment which was concerned to maintain the status
quo. He was able to see beyond that to the better order of
God's kingdom and was able to criticize the present situation

in the name of that coming kingdom. His message was full of hope and forgiveness even for the most unfortunate and desperate, with whom he gladly identified.

At the same time Jesus did not advocate violent revolution which would simply add to the evil already in the world and not change anything. Though sympathizing with the revolutionaries' analysis of what was wrong with society and in fact being mistaken for a revolutionary himself by the political leaders of his day, nevertheless Jesus did not advocate a new political regime to be established by force through revolutionary action. He called for the love of our enemies not their destruction, for forgiveness not retaliation, for readiness to suffer instead of using force, for forgiveness instead of hate and revenge. One might even say Jesus was more revolutionary than the revolutionaries, or revolutionary in a very different way. The revolution he had in mind was a radical change of heart on the part of mankind involving conversion away from selfishness and toward the willing service of God and people in general.

The fact that Jesus was not a worldly revolutionary does not mean that he withdrew from society and refused to have anything to do with its problems, like the Essenes of his day who formed the Dead Sea community. He was not an ascetic monk and did not send his followers to a desert monastery. He did not tell them to break with the ordinary business of the world to absorb themselves with self-perfection. Far from being gloomy, Jesus stressed joy and gladness in the presence of the God whose goodness was unlimited and whose grace was unconditional.

This also made him different from the Pharisees who placed such emphasis on specific acts of obedience to the Law that they lost sight of the mercy and love of God. All in all, Jesus in his lifestyle struck a unique pose. In contrast with others he lived out the message that he proclaimed about the love and grace of God toward all people.[6]

Within the framework of his message of the kingdom of God and in the context of a remarkable lifestyle, Jesus also made some tremendous claims regarding his own person. One thing that is very clear about the life of Jesus is the impact which his teaching and personal presence had on his hearers. People were constantly surprised and astonished at his authority (Matthew 7:28-29). Important people came and knelt before him, disciples accepted his call without hesitation. On one occasion a Roman centurion pointed to the fact that Jesus displayed more authority than even he could muster (Matthew 8:5-10).

The claims of Jesus were common knowledge even beyond his circle of followers. His enemies too took note of the authority which his acts and words displayed and tried unsuccessfully to break it down (Mark 11:28). Jesus knew that his authority came from heaven, and they seemed to know it too. It was rather hard to miss because of the way Jesus spoke and acted. In extending forgiveness to people, for example, Jesus presented himself as the mediator of God's grace and knew he possessed authority to exercise the prerogatives of God (Mark 2:10).

His authority also came out clearly in the way he chose to speak. His phrase "but I say unto you" and his use of the term "verily" both express his consciousness of enjoying divine authority. He did not say "thus says the Lord" as the Old Testament prophets did, but "verily, I say unto you." He did not say "the word of our God endures forever" as Isaiah did (Isaiah 40:8) but "my words will never pass away" (Matthew 24:35). The sense of authority and the self-reference of his teachings are surely remarkable and set Jesus apart from other figures in the history of religions.[7]

This sense of divine authority which Jesus displayed goes back to two things. First, he was aware of being anointed with the Spirit of God and able, as a prophet, to speak God's Word with complete certainty. Second, he possessed a deep aware-

ness of being the Son of God in a unique way. Jeremias in particular has established that Jesus used the term *abba* (which
means father or daddy in his Aramaic mother tongue) as an
address in his prayers to God. There are no other examples
of this usage in contemporary Judaism, but Jesus always ad-
dressed God in this way. The others perhaps regarded it as
child's talk, a form of expression too disrespectful to be so
used. But for Jesus *abba* expressed the filial intimacy he felt
toward his Father. As the divine Son of the Father, Jesus enjoyed a unique relationship with him, and his mission in the
world consisted in opening up the blessings of sonship to
those who believe.

Though this theme is solidly attested in all the Gospels, the
Gospel of John develops it most emphatically. Explaining
why he had performed a healing on the sabbath, Jesus said,
"My Father is always working, and I too must work" (5:17).
It was this claim to be equal with God and to be functioning
in the world as if he were God which provoked the Jewish
authorities to kill him (5:18).[8] His claims are still provocative
today. They force us to take a stand over against him and to
decide whether or not we think God was uniquely present in
him.

With his accustomed directness and acumen C. S. Lewis
puts the question to us this way:

I am trying here to prevent anyone from saying the really
foolish thing that people often say about him: "I'm ready to
accept Jesus as a great moral teacher, but I don't accept his
claim to be God." This is the one thing we must not say. A
man who was merely a man and said the sort of things Jesus
said would not be a great moral teacher. He would either be
a lunatic—on the level with the man who says he is a
poached egg—or else he would be the devil of hell. You
must make your choice. Either this man was, and is, the Son
of God: or else a madman or something worse. You can
shut him up for a fool, you can spit at him and kill him as a

demon; or you can fall at his feet and call him Lord and God. But let us not come with any patronising nonsense about his being a great human teacher. He has not left that open to us. He did not intend to.[9]

Jesus confronted the Jewish and Roman leaders with a difficult problem. His words and actions bothered them profoundly and appeared to pose a serious threat to the religious and political life of the nation. From their point of view Jesus had to be discredited and gotten rid of. He had to be proven a heretic in the eyes of religion and a traitor in the eyes of the law. This could be best accomplished by playing upon the various nuances of the term *messiah,* so this was done. There was a trial in which his claims incriminated him to the unbelieving Jews and his radical social views to the Roman authorities, and he was done away with by painful crucifixion.

Things looked rather different from Jesus' own standpoint. For one thing, he was aware of being the suffering servant of the Lord and knew of the redemptive significance of his suffering. He knew that he would suffer for the sake of others *Atone ment.* and that his death would set them free from the bondage of their sins (Mark 10:45). Not freedom from Roman tyranny, but liberation from the guilt and condemnation of sin: that would be the effect of his death when it came.

Furthermore his conviction about the redemptive value of his coming death was interwoven with a certainty of vindication even in the face of death. From passages in the Old Testament like Isaiah 53 and Daniel 7 he knew he would be triumphant even through death and receive a kingdom that could not be shaken.

Although there was much even in his lifetime to validate his claims for himself, it seems as if Jesus tied his claim to be God's anointed to God's *future* vindication of him in the resurrection. He held out to his hearers a future truth condition that would settle the truth question surrounding him. A bare claim without credentials does not carry much weight, but a claim tied to an event as public and noticeable as the resurrection carries a great deal.

The New Beginning

Jesus was put to death after a dramatic confrontation with the authorities, and the disciples were scattered. For some reason, however, the movement was not squelched but exploded into life on the basis of a release of power the early Christians connected with Jesus' resurrection from the dead.

How did the new beginning take place after such a disastrous end for Jesus? The answer which all Christians from the very first have given to that question is that the resurrection of Christ occurred, totally transforming the life-situation created by his crucifixion. Those who had hoped to get rid of Jesus' presence and influence failed dismally because Jesus returned to trouble them in a new way. Something immensely impressive must have happened shortly after Jesus' death to restore his disciples' faith in him after it had been so cruelly destroyed. According to their own account, "God has raised this very Jesus from death, and we are all witnesses to this fact" (Acts 2:32). It seems very unlikely that the Jesus movement within Judaism would have survived the execution of its leader or that there would be today, nearly two thousand years later, a Christian community numbering hundreds of millions unless something undeniably real took place.

I think it is important to recognize that the disciples were not expecting Jesus to rise from the dead even though he himself believed God would vindicate him. At his death they had in fact returned to their homes and to their former occupations. The reason for this is that in the Jewish expectation the resurrection of the dead would occur on the last day and involve everybody. It would not happen before this or involve only one person. They were not familiar with the idea that the Messiah would be raised by himself in advance of that great event, and it required a revolution in their thinking for them to accommodate to it. They were in fact completely demoralized by the death of Jesus and not filled with hope at all. So we cannot account for resurrection faith on the basis of the keen expectation of the disciples. Something objective must have happened to kindle faith in their discouraged hearts.[10]

One thing that happened was that the tomb in which Jesus had been buried was found empty on Easter morning. All four Gospels attest to that fact. This discovery did not clear away all the mystery, however, because at first people did not know what to make of it. The women first wondered if the body had been stolen, and the disciples subsequently refused to believe their report. The four accounts themselves contain several details difficult to harmonize. I am impressed with the *hmm* fact that the Gospels do not attempt to harmonize them; that in itself testifies to the honesty of the writers and the vividness of the experience.

Proof that the tomb was found empty is provided by the preaching of the resurrection in Jerusalem; it began almost immediately and with great effect. How would it be possible to claim that Jesus had been raised from the dead in the very city where he had been executed only a short time earlier unless there was solid evidence and testimony for the empty tomb? The preaching could not have gone on a single day if that fact were in doubt. The enemies of the church would have made good use of such an uncertainty and flatly denied what the early Christians were saying. But this they did not do simply because, I would suggest, they could not do it. And why do the Jewish traditions contain the charge that the disciples stole away the body except for the fact they too believed the tomb was empty? The preaching of the resurrection in Jerusalem immediately after Jesus' death is only intelligible on the basis that the grave was empty on the third day.

A convincing detail in the narratives we ought not to miss is the agreement that it was women who first discovered that the tomb was empty and reported it to the disciples. It is important to remember what the status of women was in first-century Judaism and to realize that their testimony was not considered binding in Jewish law. Why, if this account were created by the early church, would they introduce into the story such a detail which would actually detract from its authenticity in the minds of many? Obviously they would not do so. Such a detail would not be invented for effect; it would only be reported because it was true. (I also think it was God's way of saying that women are human too and of promoting their liberation through the gospel.) If it were a case of literary fabrication, the primary witnesses would certainly have been men.

In John's account there is a small detail of the resurrection I would like to call attention to because it seems to bear the marks of firsthand testimony. John describes Peter and another unnamed disciple running to the tomb and discovering the graveclothes lying there undisturbed just as though Jesus' body had passed through them. It then says that this disciple saw and believed (John 20:8). The very mention of such an ordinary detail suggests we are dealing with eyewitness material.

Just what he saw is also significant. The disciple saw that the heavily spiced graveclothes had not been torn off by a grave robber and then scattered about. They had just collapsed right where they were as if the body they had surrounded had disappeared. He realized in a flash what this meant: Jesus had been raised to newness of life. It was not like Lazarus who came forth from the tomb burdened under swaths of bandages and restored to the same earthly life. Jesus had been raised to a new dimension of existence.

Nevertheless, the discovery of the empty tomb did not by itself convince the early Christians of the resurrection of Jesus. The appearances of the risen Lord sealed their conviction. As Luke puts it, "For forty days after his death he appeared to them many times in ways that proved beyond doubt that he was alive. They saw him, and he talked with them about the Kingdom of God" (Acts 1:3). Paul does not mention the empty tomb, but he does record a list of those who encountered the risen Christ (1 Corinthians 15:5-8). Among those who saw the Lord were a group of five hundred, many of whom were still alive at the time Paul wrote and could have been interviewed on it. He was not talking about Christian experience in general, but a series of distinctive encounters in which the Lord appeared to certain individuals and groups.

It is hard to say exactly what the resurrection appearances were like. The evidence suggests some variation. Paul describes his experience on the road to Damascus in terms of an objective vision, while Luke stresses the objective and even physical character of what was seen. One thing is certain, the people who received appearances of the Lord were aware of how unique and distinctive the experience was. It was not just a case of the infilling of the Spirit discussed in circle two, but proof Jesus was alive in a new mode of existence. The appearances took place over a number of weeks in a variety of locales, and in the presence of a large number of people singly and in groups. It is not likely that they were the product of hallucination, especially when we consider that the disciples at this time were in a state of shock and depression.[11]

Over and above these evidences for the resurrection I should mention the awareness of Jesus risen which Christians have experienced from that day to this. The vast majority of believers have not been privileged to see the Lord, but they have experienced the power of the resurrection in their lives. Although the appearances continued only for a short time, Christ has never ceased to be present in the church and his relationship with us has been constant. Any person today, in addition to testing the historical proofs of the resurrection, can know its truth by yielding himself to the reality of Christ.

Faith in Christ does not involve a blind leap into the dark

because it is grounded in <u>historically verified events</u>. The historical evidence for the resurrection of Jesus, so long as it is not ruled out from the start as inherently impossible, is impressive and solid. Of course the knowledge we arrive at through historical argumentation is only probable. That is true of all the knowledge we gain in an empirical way. It falls short of the absolute certainty of mathematics. But it is the sort of knowledge we are able to operate on in all the affairs of life, and it is adequate to provide us with a sound basis for the trustful certainty of faith.

The Principle of Analogy

But can we in the twentieth century allow for the possibility of the resurrection of Jesus, a miraculous event so remote from our ordinary lives? How can we accept an event with no analogy in our experience, one which contradicts the contemporary view that history is a closed continuum of cause and effect?

In answer I would say that the principle of analogy *is* an important method for sifting data in the historical realm, but we must not allow it to exclude novelty altogether. Before a certain date there was uniform experience against a man setting foot on the moon but that doesn't imply no one has. Not to allow even the possibility that a miracle like the resurrection may occur is carrying the principle of analogy too far. <u>It amounts to an invincible atheistic presupposition that refuses to be dislodged even by good historical testimony</u>. Surely no one has the right to issue a metaphysical rule that legislates reality and excludes from the outset the possibility of the Christian claim being true. In the first three circles I have argued that there is a good possibility that God exists, and in the light of that we must also grant the possibility of miracles happening.

Under ordinary circumstances the scientist and historian are entitled to disregard claims to the miraculous, just as a lawyer operating under the law is entitled not to count on a presidential pardon for his client. Such a pardon if it came would be the free decision of the president and not something brought about by the legal skill of the lawyer. There is nothing he can do about it *as* a lawyer, but this does not mean a pardon cannot be issued. A miracle if it happens is certainly unexpected (it would not serve any purpose if it were not). But if there exists good evidence on its behalf, that evidence deserves to be evaluated and not shoved aside.

It really goes back to the empirical way of knowing things. Reality is not limited to what I have experienced personally. Our knowledge of it is enriched by what others have experienced and relate as well. Usually what they report agrees with what we would expect, but at other times it does not. On occasion it will open up new vistas. In that case we do not conclude that the report telling us of something novel must be false, but we weigh the testimony to see if it may be true.

In the case of Jesus' resurrection we have received convincing reports that a unique event has occurred; this event resists successful explanation by ordinary means; it seems natural, therefore, given its total context, to take this unique event for a fact. Not to believe it, in my opinion, is to give up on the ordinary way we gain knowledge of the world. There are some who seem willing to pay that price so as to avoid facing up to the issue of commitment, but I wonder about whether they are really honest.

What Does It Mean?

What all this means for the individual is that there is a decision to be made. There is good evidence that God has entered into our world in the person of Jesus and has a claim upon our lives. God raised Jesus to confirm and validate the pre-Easter message of Jesus and signal the fact that he *is* Lord of all. His claim to be the Son of God and his offer of forgiveness and salvation have been firmly established as true. So the next move is up to us.

If there is a God and if he wanted us to know that his authority was vested in the invitation of the gospel, he could scarcely have done a more appropriate thing than he has done in raising Christ. As Richard L. Purtill comments, "If I claim to have authority in a certain organization, strong evidence of my authority would be an ability to suspend the rules or make exceptions to usual procedures. You might meditate on the problem of how a God who never interfered with the working of the universe could establish a message from himself as authoritative."[12]

I urge you as readers, therefore, to face up to the authority Jesus claimed for himself and which now stands confirmed. Just as he called people to trust in him when he ministered on earth, so now he calls us to believe in him and to follow him.

It is impossible to be neutral about Jesus Christ. We must either accept or reject his claims. Not to decide is to decide. He does not call us to a merely verbal confession or a merely intellectual commitment, but to an unreserved decision to build our lives on Christ as a foundation (Matthew 7:21-27).

Many other implications flow from the validation of Jesus' person and authority. One of them is the assurance of salvation and forgiveness. As Paul puts it, "Because of our sins he was given over to die, and he was raised to life in order to put us right with God" (Romans 4:25). Christ saw his own death in terms of redeeming mankind from sin, and his resurrection indicates that sin has been put away and no longer stands over us to condemn us. "There is no condemnation now for those who live in union with Christ Jesus" (Romans 8:1).

Another implication relates to hope. In Jewish thought resurrection meant the salvation of the whole person in the context of a new age. For the early Christians the resurrection of Jesus filled them with hope because it was proof positive that it was possible to look beyond death to the redemption of the whole person and of creation itself. As Peter says, "Because of his great mercy he [God] gave us new life by raising Jesus Christ from death. This fills us with a living hope, and so we look forward to possessing the rich blessings that God keeps for his people" (1 Peter 1:3-4). The resurrection of Jesus enables us to live with hope amidst whatever discouraging circumstances because it assures us of God's final victory over the powers of darkness and the ultimate triumph of his kingdom.

The factual evidence for the truth of the Christian message means that the drive toward meaning (circle one), the intuition of the reality of God (circle two) and the desire to understand the world (circle three) are all well founded and capable of fulfillment. Human life is meaningful and intelligible in the light of the evidence that life is the result not of chance but of God's creative activity and has been hallowed by God's appearance in history in the person and work of Jesus Christ.

Chapter 5

Circle Five:
The Community
Basis for
Faith

The bishops at the Second Vatican Council expressed the substance of the fifth circle of credibility: "What does the most to reveal God's presence . . . is the brotherly charity of the faithful who are united in spirit as they work together for the faith of the gospel and who prove themselves a sign of unity."[1] Because of the way they were living as a new community, outsiders asked the early Christians the reason for their hope (1 Peter 3:15). Their behavior in accord with the spirit of the gospel attracted attention to their belief system and gave it credibility in the eyes of many who were seeking a new way to live and a new society to be part of. Augustine tells us that one of the things which attracted him to Christianity was the evidence of charitable patterns of behavior he saw in the church.[2]

In the first two circles I called attention to man's existential needs and the resources of Jesus Christ to meet them, and in the following two circles discussed the intellectual basis for

faith in relation to the truth question. Now it is time to recognize that an important dimension of the lostness of mankind
and its need for salvation is social in nature, the need to find
wholeness in the context of new community and the desire to
promote greater humanization in the world.

This surely explains why many young people today give
themselves so unreservedly to the newer religious cults: they
promise fellowship in a new redeemed family. Many of the
young converts testify that the cult cared for them and accepted them just as they were. Its members made them feel
part of the group so that they felt they belonged there. There
is a tremendous hunger today for simple friendship because
of the terrible erosion of the ties of human community in
Western society. Although I believe these young cult converts
could have found this fellowship in the Christian community,
the fact is they did not. Their hunger led them elsewhere, to
groups whose belief system might seem preposterous but
whose community is credible.[3]

Issues that matter to people today both in the church and
outside it go beyond the existential and the intellectual to include the political and the ethical. It is not enough to argue
effectively about philosophical and theological questions if
these arguments are not supported by a convincing manner of
life. People expect a belief system to offer brotherhood in
place of alienation; they expect the necessary stimulation to
bring about a better human society.

For a time it was hoped that technology would be able to
transform human life and bring about a happy, prosperous
world, but this has not happened. Of course technology has
made the lives of the few a lot more comfortable and free, but
it has not meant liberation for the majority of the earth's people and has not been an unambiguous blessing even to the
minority. It has indeed been the cause of a good deal of dehumanization.

More recently a great deal of hope has been placed in

political revolution as a way to the better world we long for, but here again the promise has not been realized. There is little sign of the classless and free society predicted by Karl Marx even in the countries where communism has been tried for some time.

Just because hope cannot be sustained by secular efforts in the fields of technology and ideology, however, does not compel us to abandon hope, or even to conclude that these approaches have no role to play in taking us beyond the present impasse. What it does mean is that our hope for a new human community needs to be more securely grounded, as it can be in the message the New Testament presents.[4]

The Original Revolution

Contrary to a popular misimpression the biblical message has a great deal to do with issues of society and community, justice and love. The story begins with the call to Abram to set out upon a new kind of life of dependence on God and a new pattern of behavior. God promised Abram that he would bless the whole world through him and his descendants as they were faithful to the covenant and its stipulations which were quite explicitly expounded at Sinai after the great deliverance from bondage in Egypt. God's purpose was to make out of Israel a kingdom of priests and a holy nation, a people who were pledged to live according to a new set of standards.

Although the directions God gave them at that time were not his last word on the subject (later on, from time to time, he would add to them or modify them in the light of a new situation), Israel agreed to live in the fear of the Lord and to take seriously his commandments pertaining to the whole of life in the world: justice in public affairs, mercy toward those who come off badly, respect for the other person and love toward the neighbor. This was God's original revolution, to create a unique people, not conformed to the destructive patterns of this age, but transformed in their behavior in ways that would bring healing to the creation.

Jesus picked up on this theme in his own preaching about the kingdom of God. In the period prior to the advent of God's new regime he called people to live their lives in such a way as to be a credible sign of what was coming. He spent a good deal of his time teaching them about the behavioral implications of following him, and said that, insofar as they lived in this new way, they would be salt for the earth and light for the world. People would see the difference following him would make in their lives and praise God because of what they saw (Matthew 5:13-16). His words are an expression of the biblical social strategy in which priority is placed upon the people of God representing an alternative pattern of behavior to the brokenness of man's life in sin. For Jesus the presence of new peoplehood would be an important element in the demonstration of the truth of his own claims.[5]

Jesus himself embodied the lifestyle he called for in others. It involved a total reorientation in thought and action in which a person living by faith and under the lordship of God would undertake to advocate man's cause and pursue his salvation and well-being. The love and service of mankind takes precedence over the strict observance of the law reaching out to the person who stands in need. It does not even recognize the boundary between his own group and those outside it but embraces the enemy as well; it offers forgiveness without limit to those who trespass against us because of the pardon God extended to all in his initiative in the gospel. It means reciprocal service and responsive love which reflects the character of God and the way he behaves.

All of this Jesus put into practice. His whole behavior corresponded to his own proclamation. He ministered to the weak, the sick and the neglected. He stood up for those, like women and children, who did not count in the society of his day and affirmed the dignity of those who were considered to be moral failures. He came to seek and to save the lost and not just to call the righteous. He got himself involved with those on the fringes of society, making common cause with the underprivileged and the downgraded. In all of this Jesus was not laying down a new law, but simply calling on us all to reflect in our behavior the goodness and mercy of the Father. He showed us how it was possible to practice the grace of God as well as preach it.

The apostles of Jesus were faithful to his emphasis as well. Paul made it a habit to follow up his doctrinal teaching regarding the good news with a substantial section devoted to living the new life of love and service (Romans 12—15; Ephesians 4—6). His thought is beautifully expressed in these words:

> You are the people of God; he loved you and chose you for his own. So then, you must clothe yourselves with compassion, kindness, humility, gentleness, and patience. Be tolerant with one another and forgive one another whenever any of you has a complaint against someone else. You must forgive one another just as the Lord has forgiven you. And to all these qualities add love, which binds all things together in perfect unity. (Colossians 3:12-14)

With the resurrection of Christ Paul believed a new order had dawned, an order in which a whole new set of attitudes and behaviors patterned on the example of Jesus was appropriate, including a new attitude toward the weak and a spiritual freedom from possessions.

In one of his letters Paul devotes two whole chapters to a specific case where the Christian ethic was being worked out (2 Corinthians 8—9). He wanted others in the churches to know about the action taken by the Macedonian believers. It seems that these Christians, by no means well off themselves, really sacrificed to support the beleaguered saints in Jerusalem who were suffering terrible privation.

Paul mentions two reasons why they did so. First, they were moved by the example of Christ himself who had sacrificed everything to become the Savior of mankind. No one was ever richer than the preincarnate Son of God, and none became any poorer than he was in his life on earth. His example, the classic case of voluntary self-impoverishment, simply demanded that they sacrifice too on behalf of the needy (8:9).

Second, these Christians were also concerned about justice and equality. They did not consider it fair to possess a relative abundance of this world's goods when others were suffering real want (8:14). So they did what they could to rectify the situation through a charitable donation. They did not consider what they possessed to be an inalienable right but a stewardship from the Lord for which they were responsible.

Paul explains that the reason they were not anxious about their own livelihood, even though they gave what they could ill afford, was the reality of their faith in God who richly blesses those who obey his will. They found their security in him not in worldly possessions, and that had a liberating effect upon their generosity. Paul gives the story in full because their action illustrated so well the heart of the Christian ethic: "Look out for one another's interests, not just for your own. The attitude you should have is the one that Christ Jesus had" (Philippians 2:4-5).

To sum up, the gospel in the New Testament in addition to offering everlasting life also aims at restoring the quality of life God intended us to have here and now. It includes a strong emphasis upon the development of God's people who are called to be a model community in the world as a witness to God's grace in their communal existence.

So far in this book I have tried to make the Christian message seem attractive and easy to accept. At this point, however, we run into the price that has to be paid by the one who receives it. Jesus is obviously asking for strenuous and total commitment, and that can make the gospel hard to accept.

On the other hand that may be exactly what some of you have been wanting to hear. Communism has certainly not suffered on account of the large demands it makes of party members. Something we consider of highest value can make strong demands upon us; indeed we expect it to. If the Christian message is true, then it deserves our complete commitment, and I am not ashamed of revealing this demand and placing it in full view. We are being asked to give our lives to God as a living sacrifice.

The Social Impact of the Gospel

The social impact of Jesus' message of love and service did not end with the close of the New Testament. Although the Greek philosophers exhorted people to exercise moral reason, historian W. E. H. Lecky comments:

It was reserved for Christianity to present to the world an ideal character, which through all the changes of eighteen centuries has inspired the hearts of men with an impassioned love; has shown itself capable of acting on all ages, nations, temperaments, and conditions; has been not only the highest pattern of virtue but the strongest incentive to its practice; and has exerted so deep an influence that it may be truly said that the simple record of three short years of active life has done more to regenerate and to soften mankind than all the disquisitions of philosophers and all the exhortations of moralists.[6]

On what evidence does this high praise rest? As far as the early church is concerned, church historian Adolf Harnack summarizes the evidence Lecky also presents in the form of ten specific ways in which the first generations of Christians manifested their concern for mankind.[7] (1) Liberality in almsgiving was enjoined upon them, which extended also to funds being organized to distribute money to the needy, to widows and orphans in particular. (2) Support was extended to the sick and the disabled, and hospitals were established in the major cities. (3) So effectively did the early church show their care and concern for prisoners and those languishing in the mines that Licinius, the last pagan emperor before Constantine, passed a law to prohibit anyone alleviating the suffering of these unfortunates. (4) Funds were directed to provide decent burial to the poor requiring it, a concern which made Christianity attractive to the populace which could appreciate the value of this action. (5) Although the early Christians did not yet think of trying to have slavery abolished, they did treat slaves as human beings and insisted on humane treatment for them. Often slaves were ransomed from bondage out of church funds. (6) There are numerous testimonies too concerning the way the Christians responded to need in the face of great calamity. "Alone in the midst of this terrible calamity they proved by visible deeds their sympathy and humanity. All day long some continued without rest to tend the dying and bury them—the number was immense; and there was no one to see to them; others rounded up the huge numbers who had been reduced to scarecrows all over the city and distributed loaves to them all, so that their praises were sung on every side, and all men glorified the God of the Christians and owned that they alone were pious and truly religious: did not their actions speak for themselves?[8] (7) In addition to teaching the dignity of labor, the early Christians made efforts to provide work for the unemployed and training for those without a craft. People who could not work were maintained out of church funds.

In addition to such positive steps to alleviate suffering the early Christians also condemned practices like abortion, infanticide and suicide, which cheapen life. They were unanimous in denouncing the cruelty of the gladiatorial games in the face of almost total silence on the part of the Roman writers. The games ended finally when Honorius the monk rushed into the arena to stop the games and was killed in the process.

In sum, the social impact of the early church was tremendous. Citing Lecky again:

The shadows that rest upon the picture, I have not concealed; but, when all due allowance has been made for them, enough will remain to claim our deepest admiration. The high conception that has been formed of the sanctity of human life, the protection of infancy, the elevation and final emancipation of the slave classes, the suppression of barbarous games, the creation of a vast and multifarious organisation of charity, and the education of the imagination by the Christian type, constitute together a movement of philanthropy which has never been paralleled or approached in the pagan world. The effects of this movement in promoting happiness has been very great. Its effect in determining character has probably been greater still.[9]

The church has been a creative and beneficial social force in more recent times as well. Ideas we take for granted—the need for hospitals, schools, public health, care of the mentally ill and so forth—all began as the result of Christians being concerned for such matters. Social reforms followed after. The ministry of John Wesley in Britain has been credited with the social transformation of the nation at the very time France was undergoing traumatic revolution. Similarly in North America, in the wake of revivals under Charles Finney, there was a powerful impulse of social reform affecting slavery, the status of women and the condition of the poor.[10] Other outstanding and well-known examples are the work of John Howard in prison reform, the role of the Quakers in civil and religious liberty, the ministry of the Salvation Army and so on.

The problem is not to find examples of the social impact and relevance of the Christian community, but in a short space to give anything like an adequate impression of it. There are literally hundreds of Christian relief agencies, of educational and medical efforts in connection with the world mission of the church, of agricultural and literacy projects in operation at this very moment, attempting to alleviate the needs of the earth's people.

A famous and moving symbol of what faith in Jesus can

mean in a suffering world is the stooped figure of Mother Theresa of Calcutta. She has given her life, together with hundreds of workers, to minister to the poorest of the poor, those dying in the streets in that and other cities. Less well known, but also symbolic is the charismatic prayer community in El Paso, Texas, which tries to minister to the needs of the poor who inhabit the city dump across the border in Juárez, Mexico.

Although as an individual, Mother Theresa is unique and not typical, it is significant that she gains her inspiration and vision from the church, a community founded on Jesus' own revolution of love. Although this society of Jesus often falls short, the church is still a fellowship which believes in the possibilities of love, healing and resurrection. What other community is there in the whole world which can inspire such hope and commitment?

I invite you, therefore, to participate in a community which has Jesus for its guiding principle and living model for social existence. It does not take much imagination to see how different things would be, not only for the individual but for society as well, if this message and this offer were acted on.

Christians believe that history and culture can be regenerated and transformed by the power of the gospel, and brought to a greater degree of reflection of God's purposes and glory. The document from Vatican II which I quoted at the beginning of the chapter is perhaps the strongest public statement ever made by a Christian body expressing the power of the gospel to change culture:

The Council gazes upon the world which is the theatre of man's history, and carries the marks of his energies, his tragedies, and his triumphs—that world which the Christian sees as created and sustained by its Maker's love, fallen indeed into the bondage of sin, yet emancipated now by Christ. He was crucified and rose again to break the stranglehold of the evil one, so that this world might be fash-

ioned anew according to God's design and reach its fulfillment.[11]

As for the record, Kenneth Scott Latourette concludes:

More than any other religion, or, indeed, than any other
element in human experience, Christianity has made for
the intellectual advance of man in reducing languages to
writing, creating literatures, promoting education from
primary grades through institutions of university level, and
stimulating the human mind and spirit to fresh explorations into the unknown. It has been the largest single factor
in combating, on a world-wide scale, such ancient foes of
man as war, famine, and the exploitation of one race by
another. More than any other religion it has made for the
dignity of human personality. This it has done by a power
inherent within it of lifting lives from selfishness, spiritual
mediocrity, and moral defeat and disintegration to unself-
ish achievement and contagious moral and spiritual power.
It has also accomplished it by the high value which it set
upon every human soul through the possibilities which it
held out of endless growth in fellowship with the eternal
God.[12]

BPGINFWMY

Of course it would be dishonest not to admit that there are
many blemishes too on the church's record of providing an
intimate and socially effective community. Many have had difficulty seeing much newness in her and found much to criticize. Alongside examples of loving service it is common to find
cases of stupidity and perversity. The charge is made that the
church does not usually live up to her own calling to represent
the servant presence of Jesus in the world. What is there to say
to this accusation?

First, and most fundamentally, the Christian message does
not consider the church or the individual completely redeemed but as existing in a tension set up by the conflict still

raging between the new order Jesus has initiated and the coming of the kingdom in consummated form at the end of history. The believer and his community can expect to experience warfare between his own fallenness and the powers of the age to come conveyed by the Spirit in his life. He can expect to share in the weakness and sufferings of Christ even as he seeks to follow the Lord in the world. This is the meaning of the lapel button you sometimes see: BPGINFWMY—"Be patient, God is not finished with me yet!"

Although I wish it were not so in the interests of persuading some of my readers to turn to Christ, the fact remains that the church is not yet what Christians believe it will be when God makes it a glorious church without spot or wrinkle (Ephesians 5:27). Furthermore, there are tares in the midst of the wheat as well as different qualities of soil in which the Word takes root. Until Christ returns, there are going to be people who will use the cloak of religion to cover up their own misdeeds, who will prostitute the symbols of the gospel in the service of power and greed. But Jesus does not sanction any of this, and a fair-minded person will often be able to discern between what is genuine and what is spurious.

Second, it is not easy to convince Christians that their faith consists of more than an inward experience or a creedal confession. And, having done that, it is not easy to set the churches in motion unpacking the social implications of the gospel in relation to problems which today are complex, titanic and threatening. The age of expansion with its faith in unlimited economic growth is about to give way, it seems, to a new period of scarcity and economic contraction. At the same time as we in the West are having to tighten our belts, the situation in the rest of the world is becoming grimmer. Huge disparities of wealth continue to exist and increase, and there is starvation, malnutrition and homelessness on a vast scale.

I cannot predict whether the church will rise to the task and spearhead, as she has often done in the past, the response that is needed. I know the potential is there for Christians to be the driving force in constructing alternative ways to live and act appropriately to the challenge because they have often done it before. I know that the church which exists in all countries of the world and listens to the voice of its Shepherd is capable of mounting a peacemaking and reconciling program. Already we see signs of this in the network of radical Christian communities springing up in city and countryside— living simply, serving the poor, resisting the arms race. And there are many more in the mainline churches listening to the call to downward mobility on behalf of the hungry of the world.[13]

It is not a foregone conclusion in my mind that the church will live up to its own high calling. She seems so often captive to the materialism of our age and deaf to the words of her own prophets. But I am certain that what she stands for is the most relevant option before us. Her vision of a reconciled community, called to exercise a servant ministry in the world, could not be more relevant than in an age like this when if we do not love each other we will very likely perish. It is not a question of the church taking sides with the left or with the right. She has no secret plan for the systematic reform of society, apart from practicing love in all our human relationships. Who can doubt but that tremendous social consequences will follow from humble faithfulness of that sort?

The alternative does not look hopeful. There is a strong trend in Western culture toward selfism in psychology which means a move toward the worship of the self and its interests.[14] As an alternative to following the way of Jesus, people are being lured into a life of self-indulgence and self-interest, a lifestyle which not only leads to destruction from the Christian standpoint but also guarantees that the hungry will not be fed and the needy cared for.

Set before each of us is a choice between a broad way and a narrow way. I want to challenge you to choose the narrow way: to find life by losing it in the service of God and our neighbors.

Let me bring the matter closer to home. If Jesus put so much stock upon living in the style of love he embodied and taught, perhaps we have a clue about how to test for the truth of his message and claims. After all, he said, "Whoever is willing to do what God wants will know whether what I teach comes from God or whether I speak on my own authority" (John 7:17). In other words, the person who is prepared to read the Gospels and act upon what they say can expect to receive clarification on the truth question. It may be that for some the truth will not become apparent by thinking the gospel through but by deciding to live it out.

Chapter 6

In Case
of Doubt

Even though good evidence such as I have surveyed helps us reach a reasonable certitude in regard to the truth of the Christian message, there will be times when we will be unsure about it. I am not speaking of an uncertainty which stems from changing moods and feelings, but doubt which arises from encountering data which does not seem to fit, when objections to faith seem to overwhelm faith itself.

I sympathize with those who experience difficulties which prevent them from believing or impede growth in their faith. The reason is simple: I know what it is to doubt and question. And I suspect that every Christian who takes the time to think seriously about his faith does so too. It is not necessarily the result of bad motives on the doubter's part. I say "not necessarily" because there are doubts that do represent an effort to avoid God's claim on us, but I am not talking about that kind. I am referring to doubts which come out of our quest for fuller understanding, a quest connected to the drive to want to know, which is part of our human nature.

Of course, there is also a good side to this sort of uncertainty. If we were not intellectually restless, we would not investigate things further and would not grow in our understanding. Doubt can spur deeper reflection and further discovery. The fact that you are reading this book is proof to me that you are questioning, and the reason I wrote it is so that the doubting may lead to greater certainty. Doubt can lead to good results.

There is also an objective reason why we have unanswered questions, namely, the fact that God has not revealed to us everything we would like to know. Moses said, "There are some things that the LORD our God has kept secret" (Deuteronomy 29:29). And Paul admitted, "What I know now is only partial; then it will be complete" (1 Corinthians 13:12). Think about it: if our knowledge of the things of God and of his ways with us is sufficient but partial, then it follows that we will likely be ignorant or inadequately informed on a number of subjects. Things that fall outside the circle of the light of revelation will remain obscure and may not yield their secrets even under the closest scrutiny. Clarity on them may not be given until the end of history when all will be made plain. This means that we must be true to our darkness as well as our light. There must be a place in our consciousness for modesty and even reverent agnosticism on subjects that are just not ours to know.

Job was like that. He clung to what he knew and refused to affirm what he did not. He did not have the know-it-all attitude characteristic of his friends. Aspects of his experience were confusing to him, and he was not ashamed to admit it and bring them to God. In the end God affirmed him in his questioning and Job learned to suspend judgment in the matter and trust in the Lord.

So far in the book I have been presenting the evidence that

favors the Christian position and featuring arguments which contradict the unbelieving secular standpoint. The time has come to consider some of the difficulties which arise for those attempting to establish its truth. Not considering myself to be close-minded, I want to be frank and open about that which counts *against* the Christian faith as well. It is only fair since I am asking others to do so with respect to their own commitment.

Pseudoproblems
Christians have often been their own worst enemy in the way they have invented problems for themselves that need not have arisen, not only causing themselves a good deal of anxiety but also deterring otherwise interested persons from looking into the truth question further. It usually happens when they take up strong positions where revelation is noncommittal. Their own opinions thus become obstacles in the path of other people's search for the truth. Those who have been deflected from investigating the Christian message further on account of these pseudoproblems deserve an apology.

One of these is the so-called warfare between science and religion, specifically, the debate over evolution versus creation. Even today Christians are doing battle with the scientific establishment on behalf of what is called creationism as if the Christian faith itself depended on it. Faith in the Creator does not require faith in specific details concerning His creation. The Bible does not date the creation nor describe the methods God employed in its formation. Whether it took aeons of time or a shorter period is not part of Christian essentials. It is sometimes harder for a person to consider the gospel seriously when such a concept is made a prerequisite to faith.

There are relatives as well as absolutes in Christianity, and a strict position on the age of the earth and the mechanism of the creation of man belongs to the area of relative human opinion on which it is legitimate to differ. Creationist dogma-

tism and evolutionist dogmatism are both unseemly in an
intelligent person. The discussion must go on, but a Christian
has perfect liberty to follow the evidence where it seems to
lead.[1]

A second pseudoproblem which need not trouble the in-
vestigator into the truth question surrounding the gospel has
to do with the fate of those who do not hear the gospel in their
lifetimes. There is a hard-line view on this subject which states
categorically that there is no possibility of salvation outside
an explicit faith relationship with the Jesus of the Christian
proclamation, a view which would exclude the majority of the
human race. Needless to say, this opinion has caused sensitive
Christians much pain and posed an almost insuperable bar-
rier to those who might otherwise be interested in the gospel.

There is another view, equally ancient and capable of validation from the Scriptures, that holds that God deals with
people where he finds them. If he finds them in paganism,
as he found Abraham and Melchizedek, he can communicate
with them in that milieu. God's revelation of himself is universal and the light is sufficient for those who are chrono-
logically A.D. but spiritually B.C. to respond and give themselves to God. As C. S. Lewis said, God has not revealed all his
arrangements to us, and we are not required to speculate
about the outcome of judgments God has not yet shared with
us. In this matter too we must stay within the bounds of revelation. If we do, this problem will not be insuperable.[2]

A third pseudoproblem created by Christians is the question of the date of the return of Jesus Christ. Though Scripture gives us no way to know the date and Jesus specifically
denies it is any of our business to know what the Father has
kept to himself (Acts 1:7), some have not been deterred from
trying to fix the date. I suppose this stems from a natural
curiosity coupled with an uninformed reading of the prophetic literature in the Bible. But whatever the reason, it is
wrong to tie the credibility of the Christian message to a haz-

ardous opinion which has no solid basis. The twentieth century alone is strewn with a mass of erroneous predictions in
which prophecy and current affairs have been associated,
with the result that the gospel is discredited and God's people
disillusioned.[3] There is no excuse for such date setting.

The Bible is restrained in the amount and precision of the
information it offers on a range of topics we would love to
know more about. Although our curiosity may incline us to
improve on the situation, we should resist the attempt. God
knows what he is doing in this matter. We should leave it up
to him. By giving in to the inclination we only confuse things
and possibly hinder people from facing up to the real issues.
In my experience a good number of the difficulties which
cause people anxiety are pseudodifficulties. They need not
stand in the way of a faith commitment.

Blessings in Disguise: Marx, Freud and Feminism

There is another category of difficulties which are misper-
ceived as problems for faith as well, although they are poten-
tially more serious. They appear to be frontal attacks on
religion in general and the Christian message in particular,
but in fact they are wide of their target as far at least as the
gospel is concerned. If anything they purify our understanding of faith and bring it closer to authentically biblical religion.

Take the attack Karl Marx made on religion. He said it was
the opiate of the people and that it sanctioned an unjust social
order. But he also admitted that the Bible was fully committed
to justice for the poor even if bourgeois Christianity in his
time was not. In effect, therefore, we can read Marx's position
as a challenge to get back to our own roots in the prophets and
the apostles and awake from our stupor as pillars of the unjust status quo. Marx did not really register a serious criticism
of the Christian message as I am commending it, but railed
against Christianity gone to seed, forgetful of its proper
mission.

Marx serves the church as a secular prophet to call us back to socially relevant religion contained in our own Scriptures. In Russia, Marx became the rod of God's anger against a church which had become worldly and complacent. Today Christianity in the Soviet Union is a very different force as illustrated by Aleksandr Solzhenitsyn. Marx is not a threat to my faith in Christ, but a stimulus to pursue the righteousness of the kingdom of God as Jesus taught it (Matthew 6:33).

Marx creates a difficulty for bourgeois religion, but not for the gospel of Jesus Christ. Without accepting his economic theory, which has not proven its truth, I am grateful to him and not resentful for his severe but well-appointed criticism.

The same can be said about Freud's attack on religion. He thought of belief in God in terms of an infantile projection of a person's need for security. Religion stems from wish projection, and believers are the victims of an illusion. The examples he used were the worst he could find. He certainly did not take seriously Isaiah or Amos, Jesus or Peter, Blaise Pascal or Karl Barth. It would be difficult to charge that these intellectual and spiritual giants who wrestled with the need to be critical and honest as well as devout were being deluded. Freud is guilty of willfully caricaturing all the great religions, and certainly the Christian message, which he does not seem to have bothered to try to understand.

Many of the things he said about neurotic religion, of course, were true and perceptive, but nowhere in his writings is the slightest indication that he recognized religion at its best and what it can mean to honest people every bit as intelligent as himself. His charge is wide of the mark as far as the gospel is concerned.

There is of course a sense in which the gospel is a pearl of great price, as Jesus said, because of its ability to satisfy man's hunger for meaning. But it is not simply a benefit that has no demands to make of us. It introduces a disturbance into our lives as well. Life would be much easier if it were not for the

high moral standards set by Jesus. A person who would char-
acterize faith in Christ as wish projection does not know what
he is talking about. He is just mouthing a theory without
bothering to check the evidence that supports it. He needs to
read what Pascal said in such a situation, "Let them at least
learn what is the religion they attack, before attacking it."[4]

Although Freud's attack does not achieve what he hoped,
the destruction of religion root and branch, it does perform
the valuable service on behalf of faith in exposing styles of
belief which really are neurotic and infantile. Thus, like
Marx's attack, it serves positively as a critical scalpel, cutting
away the diseased matter which often clings to the body of
true religion. Freud does not give us a reason to avoid faith
but a reason to adopt it for the right reasons.

A third example of criticism which is a disguised blessing
is raised by the secular feminist movement. Although women
have been the best friends religion ever had, it is charged that
religion has not been the best friend women have had. The
church has practiced discrimination against women in deny-
ing them the rights of full personhood and in refusing to
recognize the validity of their gifts and callings. Furthermore,
the church's language has been insensitively sexist.

Here again the charge registers against the practice of the
churches historically, but it does not threaten the gospel they
claim to be based on. Therefore, the charge amounts to a call
to reform and to return to revelational roots. The gospel message is a powerfully liberating word on behalf of women. It
guarantees their liberation from the very patterns of sexist
domination which the church has fallen into. It is not the
enemy of women's liberation but one of its most important
roots and continuing supports. Whereas secular humanism
cannot sustain the dignity and worth of persons male or
female on an adequate basis, the gospel can. "There is no difference between Jews and Gentiles, between slaves and free
men, between men and women; you are all one in union with

Christ Jesus" (Galatians 3:28).

Difficulties such as these seem to be deadly blows against the possibilities of faith, but are really not so when examined. They function like chisels chipping away the barnacles that have gotten attached to the ship of faith. They can be welcomed because of their potential to help refine and perfect our understanding of the truth. Far from being deadly blows, they sharpen our understanding of the Word of God. They act as incentives to believe the gospel just as it is and not to corrupt it by following human traditions.

Real Difficulties

Not all objections to Christian faith are unfounded or misguided. Some of them have real bite. Given the incompleteness of revelation noted earlier as well as the finiteness of human understanding, that is not surprising. At the same time I am surprised how *few* real difficulties there are, and how even these are susceptible to reasoned discussion and plausible explanation. I do not believe that because of them the Christian position is left in a worse condition than other world views; quite the contrary. Even at those difficult points the Christian message excels in pointing out possible resolutions.

One real difficulty is the problem of evil. How is it that God who is good allows such suffering and wickedness to go on in a universe over which he reigns? I suppose the great bulk of the problem can be placed on mankind's shoulders who has misused his creaturely freedom, and the reason why God allowed this to happen relates to his respect for man's relative autonomy. It is surely not a bad thing that the world is a place where the good effects of moral deeds and the bad effects of evil deeds are both allowed to run their course.

At the same time the Bible, while placing a good deal of the blame for evil squarely on man's shoulders, recognizes a mysterious dimension to the problem of evil which it does not try to explain. The first few verses of the Bible according to the best translations acknowledge the presence of a dark power of chaos which was there from the beginning. "In the beginning, when God created the universe, the earth was formless and desolate." The words that are used suggest more than simply "as yet uncreated" and give the impression of some kind of dark opposition to God's will and Word. The Bible makes little effort to elucidate the origin and precise character of this dark reality which threatens God's rule, and therefore we lack the full explanation we might like.[5]

At the same time, however, an answer is given which, although it does not explain the "genesis" of evil, does offer hope about its "exodus." The gospel itself is posited as the solution to the problem of evil. Without evil, the good news would not even be needed.

The gospel offers resources for coping with the problem of evil that cannot be matched anywhere in philosophy. It proclaims as God One who was prepared to enter into the suffering and pain of the world in Jesus Christ and Who extends to all the promise of deliverance and redemption in the event of his resurrection. The good news makes it possible for us to live in hope despite the continuing presence of evil in the world because we have glimpsed the liberation that is coming on the whole creation. So the Christian answer, if I may call it that, to the problem of evil is not found in any superior ability in philosophical reasoning, but arises out of the divine action against evil in the person and work of Christ.

Now isn't that really more important? Is it not more important for the vast majority of the human race to be able to hope even in the presence of evil rather than to be able to explain why there is a problem which nobody denies? As an elitist problem for philosophers and theologians, evil is likely to remain incompletely understood. But as a problem affecting the majority of us, it can be transformed into the shout of victory owing to the triumph of Jesus Christ. The reader must decide which is more important. If you had asked an early Christian what he thought about the problem of evil and what he proposed to do about it, he would have said without hesitation, "I believe in the good news!" I have never heard a better solution myself.

For some people a further dimension of the problem of evil is added by the Christian doctrine of hell and final judgment. Antony Flew comments dryly, "The whole issue becomes immeasurably worse if you want hell too."[6] In response, here is a word on behalf of the idea of divine judgment at the end of history.

Surely what would make the problem of evil "worse," to use Flew's term, would be for history to end without there being any day of reckoning. A world with no final judgment would be a world where injustices are never put right and evils never requited, where the enormous mountain of offenses against divine majesty and human dignity is never dealt with. If we take an ethical view of the world, then surely there must be and should be a day when the triumph of righteousness and the defeat of evil is established. Only that can make sense of the moral motions of our own hearts. Divine judgment is not only a vindication of God's justice; it is a vindication of our own too. The Christian message contains a warning of the coming judgment of God which ought to be taken seriously.

It would not be true to say, as Flew does, that anybody "wants" a hell. I think most Christians would agree with C. S. Lewis when he says, "There is no doctrine which I would more willingly remove from Christianity than this, if it lay in my power."[7] But we cannot do so for two reasons: first, because it enjoys the full support of Christ's own teaching, and second, because it makes a good deal of sense. If the gospel is extended to us for our acceptance, it must be possible also to reject and refuse it. The alternative would be for God to compel an affirmative response.

It would be nice to be able to say that all will be saved, but the question arises, Does everyone want to be saved? What would love for God be like if it were coerced? There is a hell because God respects our freedom and takes our decisions seriously, more seriously perhaps than we would sometimes wish. God wants to see hell completely empty, but if it is not he cannot be blamed. The door is locked only on the inside. It is not Christians, but the unrepentant who "want" it.

I suppose the main objection to the doctrine of hell is really influenced by the medieval imagery associated with it: flames, pitchforks, the devil in a red robe. Christians are themselves to blame for adding to the scriptural imagery and for interpreting the word pictures so literally. The purpose of the teaching is to impress upon us how terrible it will be to exist outside the presence of God. The punishment, I believe, will not be so much torment visited upon lost souls as it will be the sorrow of having chosen to play god to the end and reaping the harvest of that choice. Sinners in hell will enjoy the horrible freedom they have chosen, and there is no reason to think they would have it otherwise.

By dying on the cross Christ has done everything appropriate and sufficient to make it unnecessary for anyone to find himself in hell. I cannot see how this doctrine makes the problem of evil worse.

Dealing with Doubt

Even after you decide to accept Christ, you will still experience the problem of doubt. The Bible itself in a very frank way presents believers expressing great confusion and turmoil about the way things seem to be going in their lives. Before the complete redemption I spoke of in circle five, the Enemy of souls will be active, seeking to undermine and upset our confidence in Christ. The experience of doubt is part of the warfare going on between the kingdom of God and the old order of sin and death. Faith, even when it is supported by evidences, does not put an end to this experience of conflict.

On the other hand, God does not abandon us in such circumstances. When Thomas the disciple of Jesus refused to believe the testimony of his colleagues about the resurrection appearance of the Lord, the Lord came to him too and overcame that particular doubt, leading Thomas to make the great confession regarding Christ which is the climax of John's Gospel: "My Lord and my God!" (John 20:28). True, there is an element of rebuke too, because Thomas ought to have believed the good and sufficient evidence available to him and not insisted upon special treatment not available to us now. Nevertheless God graciously helped him in his doubt and brought him beyond it to a deeper faith commitment. I believe he will do the same for each one of us.

I have not yet mentioned the greatest difficulty of all. The majority of people do not believe in the gospel because they have a mistaken impression about who God is. Why should they believe in a God they see to be remote, arbitrary, unemotional, strict, sexist and so forth? Why would anyone expect them to be impressed with intellectual arguments for the existence of such a God, much less feel any desire to love, worship or serve him? Misunderstanding the nature of God is the greatest all-time hindrance to becoming a Christian, and understanding him correctly the greatest incentive.

There is something irresistible about the image of God presented to us in the Christian message, God with a human face. He is the One who has created us and sustained us, and wants to be our Father. His plans for us are good, and his promises embrace the whole of our need. He loves us passionately with an everlasting love and has swept away all our sins through the death of his Son. It is difficult though not impossible to reject a God like this. I don't know why anyone would.

Conclusion

I am convinced that faith needs to face up to the truth question and that the Christian message fits the facts. It is not a presupposition that has to be accepted on authority or a self-evident truth that needs no argument; it is a solid truth claim that can be tested and verified across the whole range of human experience. It meets our existential needs, makes sense out of our religious intuitions, stands up under rational scrutiny, corresponds with the historical evidence and speaks to today's moral necessities. The message is validated in all five areas of investigation and is not found wanting. It is open to examination and proves able to give an intelligible account of itself.

By speaking of five *circles* I have sought to identify for the reader five basic areas of evidences which support the Christian truth claim. Changing the metaphor, I might have described it in terms of five legs supporting a table, or five argumentative links in a legal brief, or even five strands of twine twisted together into a rope.

Like legs of a table, each shaft of evidence does its part to support the weight of the case for Christianity. Because we are all differently conditioned culturally, it is inevitable that some of us will be more impressed with one evidential approach than another. But all five have a legitimate place.

From another perspective the five circles constitute five steps of argument which build on each other and lead to the conclusion that a decision for Christ needs to be made.

If we think in terms of a rope, we notice that it is composed of strands of twine of various lengths and tension. If we were to unravel it and test the strength of the strands separately, we would not find any of them unbreakable. Some of them might even be rather weak. But when the strands are bound together in the network we call a rope, the result is very strong indeed. The strength of the rope exceeds the sum of the strength of the strands individually. The strength of the argument for Christianity is found, not in one argument set off by itself but in the binding together of many evidences which conspire to produce strong conviction and a convincing basis for faith.

In the course of this book I have tried not to overstate (or understate) the degree of rational certainty these circles of evidence achieve. I am aware that efforts in Christian persuasion have often claimed more for their arguments than the facts have warranted with the result of lessening the persuasive power they actually have. I am also aware that there is a riddle to human existence (see the book of Ecclesiastes), and that fully satisfactory answers cannot yet be given to some important questions.

At the same time, the evidences that speak for the Christian message are publically accessible and I believe impressive. We cannot wait until all uncertainty disappears before dealing with ultimate issues. A decision has to be made in spite of the risk of choosing amiss. The risk after all is greatly diminished on account of the evidential signposts indicating the truth of the gospel, and we ought to take them very seriously. It is not God's way to overpower us with undeniable demonstrations. We will wait for them in vain. In respect of our cognitive freedom, his way is to provide us with good and sufficient evidence of reasonable, persuasive force, and then to invite us to enter into the trustful certitude of faith.

In the beginning of the book I discussed our ability to discern the nature of external reality and come to a decision on the basis of factual evidence. Then I wrote the book on the basis of that assumption. But there is another facet to our human knowing that must be recognized here at the end of the book. It is that all of us, reader and writer alike, see things in the external world from our own point of view. The data reaches us through the filter of the paradigm or world view that influences our perception. At certain intervals in our lives we find we have to change or exchange one paradigm for another. The purpose behind my writing this book is to call the reader to consider making a paradigm shift, specifically, to start to view reality from a new perspective, from the position of a faith-commitment to Jesus Christ. I have tried to show reason why this ought to be done.

I am convinced that the Lord of the universe is reaching out to you. He has set his love upon you and calls you to be his covenant partner. To stay away from him (and this is certainly possible) is to lose one's life and the destiny which God has for all people. To love and trust him is the way to eternal life and the door to participating in a saving process that underlies the whole historical process. To stand beneath the lordship of Christ is not a misfortune or humiliation for you. It is rather the entrance into abundant life and an existence that is truly desirable.

Therefore, I make this appeal to you: open yourself up to God, confess your failure to live a just and holy life, and determine to follow the Lord Jesus. Act upon the evidence that stands before you and accept the saving offer that is being

extended. Respond to the invitation the Lord Jesus made:
Come to me, all of you who are tired from carrying heavy
loads, and I will give you rest. Take my yoke and put it on
you, and learn from me, because I am gentle and humble in
spirit; and you will find rest. For the yoke I will give you is
easy, and the load I will put on you is light. (Matthew 11:
28-30)

NOTES

Preface

[1]For those wishing to investigate the range of apologetic efforts on behalf of the Christian faith over the centuries, I suggest Avery Dulles, *A History of Apologetics* (Philadelphia: Westminster, 1971).

[2]For an excellent survey of recent attempts to do this from an evangelical Christian standpoint, see Gordon R. Lewis, *Testing Christianity's Truth Claims: Approaches to Christian Apologetics* (Chicago: Moody Press, 1976).

Introduction: Is There Reason Enough?

[1]For more data on this matter, see F. F. Bruce, *The Defense of the Gospel in the New Testament* (Grand Rapids: Eerdmans, 1959).

Chapter 1: Circle One: The Pragmatic Basis for Faith

[1]*Humanist Manifestos I and II,* ed. Paul Kurtz (Buffalo: Prometheus Books, 1973).

[2]Clifford Geertz develops this understanding of religion in "Religion as a Cultural System," in *The Religious Situation,* ed. Donald Cutler (Boston: Beacon Press, 1968), and in his own book *The Interpretation of Cultures* (New York: Basic Books, 1973).

[3]H. J. Blackham, *Objections to Humanism* (London: Constable, 1963), pp. 105-27.

[4]Peter L. Berger, *Rumor of Angels: Modern Society and the Rediscovery of the Supernatural* (New York: Doubleday, 1969), pp. 61-94.

[5]Blaise Pascal, *Pensées,* ed. L. Brunschvicg, trans. W. F. Trotter (New York: Modern Library, 1941), pp. 60-61.

[6]See John Hick, *Death and Eternal Life* (New York: Harper and Row, 1976), pp. 147-67.

[7]Ronald M. Green, *Religious Reason: The Rational and Moral Basis of Religious Belief* (New York: Oxford University Press, 1978).

[8]Ayn Rand, *The Virtue of Selfishness: A New Concept of Egoism* (New York: New American Library, 1964).

[9]Particularly helpful in pinpointing the precise relevance of the Christian doctrine of sin to ordinary human experience in the modern world have been the writings of Langdon Gilkey. See, for example, his *Shantung Compound* (New York: Harper and Row, 1966).

[10]Schubert M. Ogden, *The Reality of God* (New York: Harper and Row, 1966), p. 37.

[11]One of the best expositors of this argument in our generation has been Francis A. Schaeffer.

[12]C. S. Lewis, *Mere Christianity* (London: Collins, 1952), p. 118.

Chapter 2: Circle Two: The Experiential Basis for Faith

[1] H. D. Lewis, *Our Experience of God* (London: Allen and Unwin, 1959), p. 65.

[2] D. Elton Trueblood, *The Knowledge of God* (New York: Harper and Row, 1939), p. 1.

[3] Blaise Pascal, *Pensées,* ed. Louis Lafuma, trans. John Warrington (London: J. M. Dent, 1960), p. 203.

[4] Cited in Charles I. Glicksberg, *Literature and Religion* (Dallas: Southern Methodist University Press, 1960), pp. 221-22.

[5] Norman L. Geisler gives more examples in his *Philosophy of Religion* (Grand Rapids: Zondervan, 1974), pp. 13-83.

[6] See also Andrew M. Greeley, *Unsecular Man, The Persistence of Religion* (New York: Schocken Books, 1972).

[7] C. S. Lewis, *Mere Christianity,* p. 62.

[8] Charles Kraft has some insights on the way God reveals himself to people through their culture. See *Christianity in Culture, a Study in Dynamic Biblical Theologizing in Cross-Cultural Perspective* (Maryknoll: Orbis Books, 1979), pp. 239-57.

[9] For a full and authoritative presentation on this subject, see James D. G. Dunn, *Jesus and the Spirit* (Philadelphia: Westminster, 1975), pp. 11-92.

[10] William James wrote the classic in this field, *Varieties of Religious Experience* (1911).

[11] Trueblood, *The Knowledge of God,* p. 107.

Chapter 3: Circle Three: The Cosmic Basis for Faith

[1] John Calvin, *The Institutes,* ed. John T. McNeill, trans. Ford L. Battles (Philadelphia: Westminster, 1960), I (book I, chap. 5, sec. 2), 53.

[2] Walther Eichrodt, *Theology of the Old Testament* (Philadelphia: Westminster, 1967), II, 107-13.

[3] For a fuller treatment, see James Richmond, *Theology and Metaphysics* (New York: Schocken Books, 1971).

[4] John Hick discusses the major theistic proofs in his *Arguments for the Existence of God* (New York: Herder and Herder, 1971).

[5] Robert Jastrow, "Have Astronomers Found God?" *New York Times,* 25 June 1978.

[6] See Bernard J. F. Lonergan, *Insight, A Study of Human Understanding* (New York: Harper and Row, 1978).

[7] C. S. Lewis, *Christian Reflections* (Grand Rapids: Eerdmans, 1967), p. 89.

[8] In this connection, see Wolfhart Pannenberg, *What Is Man?* (Philadelphia: Fortress Press, 1970).

[9] See H. P. Owen, *The Moral Argument for Christian Theism* (London: Allen and Unwin, 1965).

[10]Karl Rahner, *Foundations of Christian Faith* (New York: Seabury, 1978), p. 69.

Chapter 4: Circle Four: The Historical Basis for Faith

[1]See James D. G. Dunn, *Unity and Diversity in the New Testament: An Inquiry into the Character of Earliest Christianity* (London: SCM, 1977).

[2]Rudolf Augstein, *Jesus, Son of Man* (New York: Urizen Books, 1977).

[3]J. A. T. Robinson, *Redating the New Testament* (London: SCM, 1976).

[4]Joachim Jeremias, *New Testament Theology, The Proclamation of Jesus* (New York: Scribner's, 1971), p. 37. In another book, J. A. T. Robinson asks why the principle has to be limited to the synoptic tradition when it could also be said of John's Gospel (*Can We Trust the New Testament?* [Grand Rapids: Eerdmans, 1977], p. 132).

[5]See A. N. Sherwin-White, *Roman Society and Roman Law in the New Testament* (Oxford: Clarendon Press, 1963).

[6]For an excellent presentation of the lifestyle Jesus adopted, see Hans Küng, *On Being a Christian* (London: Collins, 1976), pp. 177-277.

[7]See James D. G. Dunn, *Jesus and the Spirit*, pp. 76-82.

[8]For a presentation of Jesus' self-understanding, see I. H. Marshall, *The Origins of New Testament Christology* (Downers Grove: InterVarsity Press, 1976).

[9]C. S. Lewis, *Mere Christianity*, pp. 52-53.

[10]For a discussion of the resurrection in Judaism, see G. E. Ladd, *I Believe in the Resurrection of Jesus* (Grand Rapids: Eerdmans, 1975), pp. 51-59.

[11]James Dunn discusses the nature of the resurrection appearances in *Jesus and the Spirit*, pp. 95-134.

[12]Richard L. Purtill, *Thinking about Religion* (Englewood Cliffs: Prentice-Hall, 1978), p. 70.

Chapter 5: Circle Five: The Community Basis for Faith

[1]*Pastoral Constitution on the Church in the Modern World*, sec. 21 in *Documents of Vatican II*, ed. Walter M. Abbott (New York: Guild Press), p. 219.

[2]Augustine, *Confessions*, book 8.

[3]Harvey Cox spent time in these groups and tells about his impressions and observations in *Turning East: The Promise and Peril of the New Orientalism* (New York: Simon and Schuster, 1977).

[4]Hans Küng has written a masterful book advancing this thesis, simply entitled *On Being a Christian* (London: Collins, 1977).

[5]For more on the social relevance of Jesus, see John H. Yoder, *The Original Revolution* (Scottsdale: Herald Press, 1971) and *The Politics of Jesus* (Grand Rapids: Eerdmans, 1972).

[6]W. E. H. Lecky, *History of European Morals from Augustus to Charlemagne*

(New York: Braziller, 1955), II, 8-9.

[7]A. Harnack, *The Expansion of Christianity in the First Three Centuries* (New York: Putnam's, 1904), I, 190-249.

[8]Eusebius, *Ecclesiastical History,* IX, 8.14.

[9]Lecky, *History of European Morals,* II, 100-01.

[10]See Donald Dayton, *Discovering an Evangelical Heritage* (New York: Harper and Row, 1976).

[11]*Pastoral Constitution,* p. 200.

[12]Kenneth Scott Latourette, *Advance Through Storm* (New York: Harper and Row, 1945), pp. 480-81.

[13]It is Jeremy Rifkin's thesis that the evangelical community is capable of launching a response adequate to the challenges we face: *The Emerging Order: The Great Economic Transformation and the Second Protestant Reformation* (New York: Putnam, 1979).

[14]See Paul Vitz, *Psychology as Religion: The Cult of Self-Worship* (Grand Rapids: Eerdmans, 1977).

Chapter 6: In Case of Doubt

[1]In this connection consult Richard H. Bube, *The Human Quest: A New Look at Science and the Christian Faith* (Waco: Word, 1971); Robert C. Newman and Herman J. Eckelmann, Jr., *Genesis One and the Origin of the Earth* (Downers Grove: InterVarsity Press, 1977); and L. Duane Thurman, *How to Think about Evolution,* 2nd ed. (Downers Grove: Inter-Varsity Press, 1978). Thurman's book helps set the whole controversy in perspective and, rather than drawing a conclusion, suggests how the quest itself should be conducted.

[2]For more on this subject see J. N. D. Anderson, *Christianity and Comparative Religion* (Downers Grove: InterVarsity Press, 1970), pp. 91-111; and Charles Kraft, *Christianity in Culture,* pp. 253-57.

[3]See Dwight Wilson, *Armageddon Now!* (Grand Rapids: Baker, 1977).

[4]Cited by Elton Trueblood who has some fine comments to make regarding both Marx and Freud in his *Philosophy of Religion,* chaps. 12—13.

[5]Barth offers a deep treatment of it but does nothing to take away the veil. See his section "God and Nothingness" in *Church Dogmatics* (Edinburgh: T. and T. Clark, 1961), III/3, 289-368.

[6]Antony Flew, *God and Philosophy* (London: Hutchinson, 1966), p. 56.

[7]C. S. Lewis, *The Problem of Pain* (London: Collins, 1940), p. 106.